VEGAN
RESET

VEGAN RESET

The 28-DAY PLAN to Kickstart Your Healthy Lifestyle

KIM-JULIE HANSEN

HOUGHTON MIFFLIN HARCOURT

BOSTON   NEW YORK   2018

Copyright © 2018 by Best of Vegan LLC

Photography copyright © 2018 by Best of Vegan LLC

Illustrations: fruit and vegetables © Mary Zabaikina / Creative Market
graphic patterns © Irene Demetri / Creative Market
watercolors © Katherine Roberts / Creative Market

For information about permission to reproduce selections
from this book, write to trade.permissions@hmhco.com or to Permissions,
Houghton Mifflin Harcourt Publishing Company, 3 Park Avenue,
19th Floor, New York, New York 10016.

hmhco.com

Library of Congress Cataloging-in-Publication Data
Names: Hansen, Kim-Julie, author.
Title: Vegan reset : the 28-day plan to kickstart your healthy lifestyle /
Kim-Julie Hansen.
Description: Boston : Houghton Mifflin Harcourt, 2018. | Includes
bibliographical references and index.
Identifiers: LCCN 2018001644 (print) | LCCN 2017058733 (ebook) | ISBN
9781328453549 (ebook) | ISBN 9781328454034 (trade paper)
Subjects: LCSH: Vegan cooking—Recipes. | Vegetarian cooking. | LCGFT:
Cookbooks.
Classification: LCC TX837.H345 2018 (print) | LCC TX837.H345 2018
(ebook) |
DDC 641.5/636—dc23
LC record available at https://lccn.loc.gov/2018001644

Book design by Laura Palese

Printed in China

SCP 10 9 8 7 6 5 4 3 2 1

Contents

Part

ONE

Getting
Started

my STORY

The book you are holding in your hands
is a cookbook, a 28-day meal plan, and a practical
guide to a vegan lifestyle. It is meant to
introduce you to the basics of plant-based cooking
and living, step by step.

WHETHER YOU ARE already vegan and simply want to learn how to prep meals and live a more balanced life, or you are brand-new to this lifestyle, or you are a meat-eater looking to kickstart healthier habits, this book is for you. I am probably one of the most unlikely people to be writing it, but I believe that this also makes me the perfect person to reach those who are struggling in the way I have struggled for most of my life. Today, I love eating healthy food and sharing my passion for this lifestyle with my friends and family, as well as people online. I write a vegan blog called *Brussels Vegan* and run an online cooking platform called *Best of Vegan*, and nothing brings me more joy than teaching others what I wish I had known years ago, as health wasn't always a priority for me.

I grew up hating fruits and vegetables and craving fast food every single day. When I was ten, I switched schools and started being bullied. As a consequence, I would isolate myself and overeat to feel better. I started gaining weight rapidly and food became my drug of choice. I continued to struggle with my weight well into adulthood. I don't have memories of wearing summer dresses and just feeling good and happy in my teens and early twenties, because those moments never happened for me. Instead, I spent my adolescence numbing my emotions by eating more, chain-smoking, and drinking.

I ate because I felt insecure, and the more I ate, the more insecure I felt. At fourteen, I started smoking and drinking in order to fit in so that the other kids at school would stop bullying me. It worked, but I started losing myself more and more and the cycle of self-sabotage seemed endless. All this time, I wanted to change, lose weight, get better. I read magazines that told me to simply go outside and run a few miles, but even that seemed impossible to me. I often wonder why I didn't find my way to veganism and a holistic

lifestyle much sooner. But I also understand that it is very difficult to get out of a state in which you believe that you'll never be able to feel better. I was so used to being unhappy and overweight that I couldn't even imagine what it would feel like *not* having to struggle. Over the years, I tried every single diet I could find in a desperate attempt to lose the weight and with it, my insecurities. The results, however, were only ever temporary, and most important, none of them allowed me to deal with the root problems that stemmed from never feeling good enough.

Over the years, I wanted to find *the* solution, a quick fix, a magic pill to make me skinny and happy. I read countless books on nutrition and exercise until I became a self-proclaimed expert on the topic, and yet, I still could not keep the weight off. The root problems of my weight issues were much deeper, so as long as I was still dealing with those, there was no way for me to find lasting peace. After high school, I decided to work for a couple of years before starting college, and by the time I started my freshman year, I was a chain-smoking, overeating, overall unhappy person, constantly living in denial and hoping to one day find my way out of the mess I had created for myself.

In 2010, when I was twenty-two years old, my father died unexpectedly of a heart attack at age fifty-three. When he died, he was severely overweight, overworked, and had been smoking two packs of cigarettes every single day for decades. Instead of taking his death as a warning sign, I thought that I, too, was doomed, and things got a lot worse before they got better. I spent the next year pretending I was fine, while numbing myself with more food, more cigarettes, more drinks. Then, in 2011, doing research about the meat and dairy industries for an essay in college motivated me to become an ethical vegan overnight. I was used to eating junk food every day and I loved meat, cheese, and eggs, so this came as a surprise to everyone, including me. Little did I know that it would turn out to be the best decision of my life. Over the next year, I started reading every book, article, and blog on veganism I could get my hands on. I watched documentaries and listened to interviews, and the more I learned, the more fascinated I became.

After starting off as a so-called "junk food vegan," I slowly taught myself how to adopt a healthier diet. The problem was that I didn't know where to start or how to put my newfound knowledge into practice. I'd always had a passion for cooking, so that was where I started experimenting, and step by step, I taught myself the skills I needed in order to succeed in this lifestyle.

Vegan Reset is the book I would have wanted to help me navigate through everything that seemed so overwhelming at first. It is written for anyone who feels like they want to improve their health and live a happier life but doesn't know where to start, for those who want to go vegan but have no idea *how* to actually do it, and for people who are already vegan but would like to know how to cook more healthy and delicious meals or how to prepare their meals in a more practical way. *Vegan Reset* will guide you through 28 days of healthier eating, with easy-to-follow shopping lists, prep instructions, and recipes. It will also teach you all you've ever wanted to know about blending, juicing, fresh produce, how to save money on a plant-based diet, and much more. In addition, it follows a holistic approach, taking into consideration that our overall well-being depends on much more than just the food we eat—exercise, sleep, and self-care are part of the picture, too. This lifestyle allowed me to feel better than I've ever felt before and to get rid of the allergies and chronic migraines I'd been suffering from for most of my life. Most important, however, this journey helped me become a happier person.

WHAT IS A RESET?

Think of a "reset" in the same way you would think of a reset button that you press to restart a device that stopped working the way it should. Much in the same way as technical devices, our bodies sometimes stop working properly if we don't give them the love and attention that they need and deserve. The problem is that when it comes to our bodies and our overall well-being, we often ignore the signs and don't think to give ourselves a break and press that button. During the Vegan Reset, you'll be doing just that, as well as receiving tools that you'll be able to incorporate into your day-to-day life well beyond the 28 days. So why should you do the Vegan Reset?

Looking for Something New?

The Vegan Reset is perfect for anyone looking to switch things up in a healthy way and try something new. The 28-day time frame lets you try out the benefits of a vegan diet without committing to a permanent change. But once you get the hang of this diet, additional recipes offer you plenty of delicious reasons to continue beyond the reset.

HOW TO USE THIS BOOK

The beauty of the Vegan Reset is that you decide what you're ready for. Many people shy away from veganism because they feel too much pressure. Feeling like you have to commit to something for the rest of your life can feel incredibly overwhelming and scary. When I first started learning about veganism, the thought of ever going vegan myself seemed extreme and intimidating. Imagine if someone were to tell you that from today on, you would have to change most of your habits and that there was no way back. How would that feel? Being expected to make changes and commit to them 100 percent from day one can feel intimidating. We are creatures of habit, and the things we're used to doing provide comfort and a sense of security, so it's only normal that the idea of losing any of that is scary. If, however, you were told to give something a try for a day, a week, or a month? That's not so scary.

The same goes for the Vegan Reset. If right now, you don't have any desire to go vegan permanently, but you just want to hit the "reset" button, that is absolutely fine. Take it one step at a time and be kind and patient with yourself. I recommend reading Part 1 of the book first and then starting the program whenever you feel ready. The 28-day plan includes advance meal prep, which requires some time at the beginning of each week but subsequently makes your daily cooking much faster and easier. The additional recipes in Part 4 of the book are meant as a resource for you beyond the 28-day program and as inspiration to start creating your own dishes.

Looking to Go Vegan?

If you've been thinking about adopting a vegan lifestyle but don't know where to begin, the Vegan Reset is the perfect program for you. The meal plan will make the first four weeks as easy as possible for you—just follow the instructions day by day. But you'll also be provided with plenty of information on this lifestyle as a whole, from how to store produce to how to travel and eat out as a vegan to how to handle social situations. As you embark on your journey, the Vegan Reset has you covered and you'll feel empowered at every step.

Looking to Go One Step Further?

If you're already vegan but want to incorporate more healthy and easy-to-prepare dishes or perhaps learn more practical tips on how to succeed long-term, you'll find just what you're looking for here. This program meets you where you are and helps you take it one step further, with an abundance of easy, delicious recipes and practical advice.

A FEW THINGS TO KEEP IN MIND

As you embark on the Vegan Reset journey, here are the key points and reminders to keep in mind.

WHY VEGAN?

The term "vegan" means not consuming or using any animal products or by-products. When it comes to food, this means no meat, seafood, dairy products, eggs, or honey (for a more thorough breakdown, see Part 3, beginning on page 138). There are many reasons to go vegan, including environmental stewardship and advocating for the ethical treatment of animals, but many people are motivated by the health benefits of a plant-based diet. Trading animal products for plant-based foods means eating fewer unhealthy fats and more healthy fats, fiber, and nutrients. You may find that on a vegan diet, you have more energy and better digestion, and you lose weight. I personally suffered from migraines, chronic headaches, and allergies for years, but after switching to a healthier plant-based diet, those gradually went away.

Eat an Abundance of Fresh Plant-Based Foods

The Vegan Reset is about abundance, not restriction. It's about eating a large variety of fruits, vegetables, starches, legumes, herbs, nuts, seeds, and spices that will give you the nutrients and energy you need. I give you filling and nutrient-dense meals for breakfast, lunch, and dinner, plus snacks so you stay satisfied all day long. It's important to make sure you eat enough, which can be challenging if you're used to restricting your portion sizes. Remember that while many animal products are high in calories and low in volume, plants tend to be the opposite—high in water content and volume but lower in calories—so you can eat more. It's about giving your body what it needs and eating for your own well-being, not calorie counting.

Keep an Open Mind

As you incorporate more plant-based meals, you may come across certain foods that are not to your liking or face unexpected challenges. All I'll ask you to do is keep an open mind. Our taste buds sometimes need ten to fifteen days to get used to new tastes, so it may take a little time for you to adapt. Be patient and kind with yourself during the process.

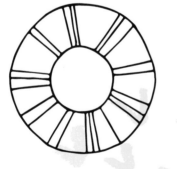

Progress, Not Perfection

It is so important to let go of the idea that unless we are "perfect," we are worthless. *Vegan Reset* is about celebrating every step, no matter how small. If you're used to spending your evenings in front of the TV, drinking liters of soda and eating chips, then something as seemingly insignificant as adding a green smoothie to your morning routine is a huge step. I know, because I've been there. I know how difficult it can seem to change your habits, especially when you rely on them to comfort you. *Vegan Reset* is meant to be your guide and confidante, something to encourage and applaud you when you yourself have a hard time believing in your ability to change and feel better.

If you miss a meal or have an off day, that's okay, just keep going. Instead of focusing on whatever it is you think you're not doing well or well enough, think of all the progress you're making and feel good about that. One of my favorite sayings is "You can't hate yourself into a version of yourself you can love." The same goes for the thoughts you think about yourself. Negative self-talk only breeds more negative self-talk and brings about negative emotions. If your goal is to feel good about yourself, then the only way to achieve that is by being your own number-one fan.

The only things you'll have to do to get ready for Day 1 of the Vegan Reset are your food shopping one or two days before and keeping an open mind. While you can buy condiments and staple foods well ahead of time, make sure you don't get the fresh produce too far in advance so that it stays as fresh as possible.

Planning is a big part of the Vegan Reset. Prepping some of the components ahead of time will make it quicker to make each meal, and also easy to pack and transport the components, if, for example, you're taking them to work for lunch. If you end up skipping one of the meals on the program, for example if you buy your lunch or go out to dinner with friends, try to make it vegan if you can, then just continue with the next meal in the plan.

One of the most important things during this experience is to not be too hard on yourself. Do the best you can and celebrate every step. Remind yourself what you're doing this for and see it as an opportunity to give yourself another chance.

What to Expect

When you go vegan, a lot of things change. When you change your diet, your body needs time to adapt. This is a good thing, as cutting out all animal products and switching to healthier whole foods means cutting out many toxins. But if at all possible, try to get a little more rest. You also might notice improved digestion. Since animal products don't contain any fiber, a lot of people are used to having very slow digestion. Fiber-rich plant-based foods are very likely to change that! During the Vegan Reset, try to observe any changes that may occur and be attentive to your needs. Resting and drinking a lot of water always helps.

Detoxification

Detoxification, or "detox," has become a very popular and trendy topic, and the term is often used to promote cleanses and supplements. The most important thing to note here is that our bodies detoxify themselves as part of the digestive process. Whenever you switch to a different lifestyle, there can, however, be a period of adjustment, which some people describe as "symptoms" like fatigue, headaches, and faster digestion. Exposing your body to less-processed foods makes digestion easier, which in turn allows it to spend more energy on its own detoxification. So when people talk about "detox symptoms," what they're really referring to are the body's own mechanisms and the way in which it is adjusting. The symptoms you'll experience, if any at all, depend on factors like your current diet, but the experience also varies from person to person. These symptoms won't last long, and some people may not experience any symptoms at all.

PHYSICAL SYMPTOMS YOU MAY EXPERIENCE

Fatigue As your body detoxifies itself, it will need a lot of energy and it will want to recuperate by sleeping more. Everyone is different and you may not feel tired at all, so just be attentive to your body's needs.

Headaches Many animal products, especially the ones that are heavily processed, can be highly addictive and you may get headaches when you stop consuming them. If that's the case, drink lots of water and make sure you get enough rest.

Quicker digestion Animal products contain no fiber, so it can take up to a few days, or in some cases even longer, to digest them. That may be the norm for many people, but it's certainly not healthy. So, if you find yourself having to go to the bathroom a little more often, view it as a good thing and a sign that your body is getting healthier.

Amazing things Some changes may take a little longer than a week, but your body can undergo amazing changes as a consequence of adopting a plant-based diet. You may also feel overall more energized, so simply stay attentive and try to enjoy the experience.

Weight Gain & Weight Loss

Veganism is an ethical stand, not a diet. Going vegan is therefore not a guarantee for either weight loss or weight gain, but a plant-based diet can be used as a tool to achieve either.

Can you gain weight and even build muscle on a plant-based diet? Yes, absolutely. There are plenty of vegan athletes and bodybuilders who continuously prove that eating plants does not have to mean losing muscle mass. You will, however, have to be mindful as you adapt your diet. Depending on what you're used to eating at the moment, you may need to increase your portion sizes or prioritize high-calorie foods. Fresh produce is higher in volume and water content than meat, dairy, eggs, and a lot of processed foods. In a nutshell:

Eat more As easy as that may sound, some people have difficulty estimating how much food they need to eat in order to consume sufficient calories to gain or maintain their weight. Luckily, there are plenty of free tools available online, like cronometer.com, that can help you track your caloric intake.

Don't be afraid of fat Nutrient-dense sources of fat such as avocados and nut butters will be the easiest and healthiest way to add more fat to your diet. You can add them to smoothies, soups, and salads or enjoy them as a snack.

Consider prioritizing strength over cardio training Cardiovascular exercise makes you lose weight a lot more quickly, so if you're looking to gain weight, consider reducing, without necessarily eliminating, the amount of cardio you do.

Losing weight is quite simple in theory, but simple certainly doesn't mean easy. It is often the emotional barriers that make it so frustrating and hard to achieve our goals. There are, nonetheless, a few practical things to keep in mind:

Go for fat loss, not just weight loss Many diets promise you unrealistically quick results, but the problem is that any weight you lose so quickly is usually just water weight or sometimes even muscle tissue. Furthermore, one pound of fat may weigh the same as one pound of muscle, but they don't have the same volume, which means that two people of the exact same height and weight can look very different from each other. This means that it's important not to pay too much attention to a number on a scale. A better indication of progress is measuring your body fat percentage or seeing how well your clothes fit and how good you feel.

Count calories as an optional tool Should you count calories in order to lose weight? The most important thing to keep in mind is that counting calories is not the same thing as restricting calories. I absolutely do not condone restricting your calories, and I think that any program or diet that focuses on reducing calories to an extreme is potentially dangerous. Counting calories should be viewed as an optional tool that you can use when you feel like you're eating the right amounts of food but are still gaining weight. Keeping track of how much you're consuming can help you gain insight and make adjustments accordingly.

Avoid emotional eating If losing weight is simple, why is it hard for so many people? Over- (and under-) eating can be linked to many deeper emotions and issues. Gaining weight can be a way to protect yourself, or eating can be a way to numb your feelings. In one of his audio programs, motivational speaker Tony Robbins mentions the example of a man who used his weight as a shield. Doing this allowed him to blame any rejection on his weight instead of on himself. I myself have used food, cigarettes, and alcohol to numb my emotions in the past. This is a way to avoid dealing with pain, but it can lead you to become passive and to live in the realm of "what if" and "maybe one day" instead of addressing your goals in the present. Exploring any deeper issues is the first step in overcoming them.

That said, not everyone who is unhappy with their weight or shape necessarily has emotional issues. Sometimes it really is just the result of circumstances, uninformed choices, or a mix of it all. Something I want to make very clear is that weight loss is not a must or a prerequisite for happiness. I believe that you can be happy and beautiful no matter your size or shape. Focus on feeling healthy and happy instead of looking a certain way. The good news is that you always have the power within yourself to change right here, right now. Here are a few practical tips that can help you become healthier and fitter on a vegan diet:

- Stay hydrated
- Eat an abundance of unprocessed, whole, plant-based foods
- Slow down and eat mindfully
- Stay away from soda, especially diet soda
- Avoid refined sugar
- Stay active and keep moving
- Get plenty of rest

STOCKING YOUR KITCHEN

Useful Kitchen Tools

Certain tools and appliances can make preparing your food easier and will undoubtedly make your time in the kitchen more enjoyable, too. I've divided them into the "essentials"—those you'll be likely to use on a daily basis and that will have the biggest impact convenience-wise—and the "extras."

....
THE ESSENTIALS

Food processor This is great for chopping vegetables, herbs, and nuts and making sauces and raw desserts. It is more convenient than a blender for shredding and chopping, as well as for getting a chunkier consistency when making sauces. If you have a limited budget and are looking to only add one appliance, I'd recommend starting with a food processor. You can find powerful ones for as little as $30. If that's still too much of an expense or you are working with limited kitchen space, then the next best thing would be an immersion stick blender, which you can find for as little as $10. That is what I used to make smoothies in college and while it wasn't ideal, it was a lot more powerful than you'd think and also allowed me to blend soups and chop herbs.

Blender (preferably high-speed) While you can definitely use a food processor or immersion blender to make smoothies, the very best results will always be achieved using a high-speed blender. Unfortunately, these tend to be very expensive, with the highest-end models ranging between $500 and $800. Luckily, you can find secondhand or refurbished high-speed blenders for $100 to $300, and some online department stores allow you to pay in installments. That is still an investment, but definitely worth it long-term. In the meantime, a cheaper version will do the trick even if the results won't be quite as smooth.

Bottom line If you can, invest in quality that will last you a very long time, but if that's not an option for you at the moment, you can still make it work with the alternatives listed previously.

....
THE EXTRAS

Juicer The two most popular types are centrifuges and slow juicers. You'll find out more about which one might be the best for you in the section about juicing beginning on page 166, but in a nutshell, the best juicer is the one you'll actually use. A slow juicer may be able to preserve more nutrients, but if you choose a model that takes forever to juice and/or clean, you may be less likely to use it and it won't be the best option for you.

Citrus press A fantastic addition to your kitchen if you're planning on making a lot of orange, tangerine, or grapefruit juice or if you're looking for an affordable alternative to a juicer. The advantage of a citrus press over a juicer is that it will preserve most of the fiber, making the citrus juice healthier and less likely to spike your sugar levels too quickly. It also saves a tremendous amount of time compared to manually juicing oranges and other citrus fruit.

Spiralizer The ultimate way to make eating vegetables more fun. You can use it to make zucchini, carrot, or even sweet potato "noodles" that can be eaten raw or steamed. Spiralizers usually only cost $5 to $40 depending on the brand and model you choose. I especially recommend this for people who are not used to eating fruits and vegetables or who dislike them. Changing the shape of the vegetables makes a big difference!

Pressure cooker (preferably electric) A pressure cooker (like an Instant Pot) is the ultimate time-saver in the kitchen. Cook beans in just fifteen minutes instead of 1 to 4 hours, and quinoa in as little as one minute. I recommend an electric model over a stovetop version for convenience and safety. Some electric pressure cookers also have sauté and slow cooker functions.

Dehydrator A dehydrator removes most of the water from fruits and vegetables to help you make snacks that are lighter and that will keep longer. You can find affordable multifunction dehydrators for under $100 and sometimes even $50 that are more compact than their expensive counterparts. Dehydrators can make many raw dishes more flavorful and make delicious healthy snacks like kale chips. The main disadvantage is that it takes a very long time, from a few hours to up to one or two days, to dehydrate produce. If you're not planning on using it regularly or if you have limited space, it might be a better idea to simply buy already dried fruits and vegetables. If, however, you like experimenting in the kitchen and/or have a passion for raw vegan gourmet dishes, a dehydrator is worth looking into.

Reusable containers and utensils Glass containers and jars and stainless steel lunch boxes are the most eco-friendly ways to store your staple foods, meal prep, leftovers, and on-the-go breakfasts and lunches. Also make sure you only use glass or stainless steel straws. Hundreds of millions of plastic straws are used and disposed every single day, which is very harmful to the environment and 100 percent preventable given the amazing reusable and eco-friendly straw options that exist today. The same goes for plastic utensils. If you can, try to travel with a reusable utensil and straw set and ask for your food or drinks to be served without plastic straws and utensils. Some eco-conscious businesses have started replacing their plastic straws with biodegradable paper straws or choose to simply omit straws. Let management know that you appreciate eco-friendly practices, or, if they're still using plastic, ask them to consider alternatives. Every step counts.

FILLING YOUR FRIDGE & PANTRY

For the 28-day reset, I give you shopping lists for the start of each week, so you can buy exactly what you'll need, without guesswork or wasting food. Some things, like olive oil, spices, and other seasonings, are staples that will last a long time—once you stock your pantry, you will need to replenish them only occasionally.

The recipes in this plan and those that follow, starting on page 154, feature abundant fresh produce and plants that are nutrient-dense. Our bodies need a combination of three macronutrient groups—protein, carbohydrates, and fat—for energy, plus micronutrients such as vitamins and minerals to stay healthy. While many diets cut out one or more macronutrient groups, like fat or carbohydrates, we actually need them all. Our bodies crave and need nutrients, not just calories per se. That is why many people can eat large amounts of processed and fast foods without feeling satiated. Those foods taste good but contain very few nutrients, which is why they're often referred to as "empty calories." For example, two Oreo-style cookies have approximately the same amount of calories as a medium banana, but a banana is more nutrient-dense and more filling. This means that it's not just about how much you eat, but above all, *what* you eat.

Here is a rundown of some of the nutrient-dense plants that will serve as your staple foods during and hopefully well beyond the Vegan Reset.

"Since the foods Americans consume are so calorie-rich, we have all been trying to diet by eating smaller portions of low-nutrient foods. We not only have to suffer hunger but also wind up with perverted cravings because we are nutrient-deficient to boot."
—Joel Fuhrman, doctor and nutrition expert

FRESH PRODUCE

Eating an abundance of fresh fruits and vegetables is the best way to maximize your nutrient intake and to stay hydrated throughout the day. They'll make you feel better overall and will increase your energy levels.

FRUIT RIPENESS

When you eat fruit, make sure it is ripe enough, as ripe fruit is sweeter and its flavor is much fuller and more intense. It also contains more antioxidants and is easier to digest. Most important, you'll be able to absorb more of its nutrients. You'll be able to tell if a fruit is ripe by looking at it, smelling it, and/or touching it. Most fruits will turn from green (because of their chlorophyll) to a brighter color like orange, yellow, or red and won't have a distinct smell unless they're ripe. Fruits like mangoes and peaches should be soft but not too soft. The more intense the color, the better. Here are a few more examples:

Avocados They should be soft to the touch, and if you remove the dry stem at the bottom, the color should be a yellowish green. If it's brown, it's already overripe.

Bananas Bananas are ripe when they're covered in spots and smell sweet.

Cantaloupe You should be able to press into it slightly. If it's too hard, it's not ripe yet. It should also smell very sweet.

Cherries The stems should still be attached and the cherries should be dark red and firm. If they're too soft, they're past their prime.

Cucumbers A ripe cucumber should be firm to the touch and medium to dark green in color. You want to stay away from a cucumber if you notice any yellowish areas or dark spots or if it smells foul.

Oranges Their skin should look bright and firm. If they're too pale, they're not ripe yet, and when the skin looks "leathery," they're overripe.

Persimmons They may look ripe when you buy them, but they can take up to two, three, or even four weeks before they're ready to eat. They should be very soft to the touch and have an almost pudding-like consistency. If they're unripe, they'll be hard and chalky and won't taste good at all.

Pineapple Unripe pineapples have no scent; ripe pineapples smell sweet; and overripe pineapples smell vinegary. The skin should be orange/yellow (no longer green), the leaves should be dark green, and you should be able to easily remove the top by twisting it. It should also be quite heavy (which means it's juicier).

Strawberries If they are white around the stem, they were picked too early and aren't ripe yet. The leaves should be dark green and not dried out.

LEAFY GREENS & SALAD GREENS

Leafy greens are among the most nutrient-dense plants and you should incorporate them into your meals whenever you can. The darker the green, the more nutrient-dense it is. I use them in salads, smoothies, juices, bowls, or as a side dish. Leafy greens must be refrigerated in order to stay fresh.

Arugula

Butter lettuce

Dandelion greens

Collard greens

Iceberg lettuce

Kale (Tuscan kale, curly kale)

Mustard greens

Romaine lettuce

Radicchio

Rainbow chard

Rapini

Spinach

Swiss chard

Watercress

FRESH HERBS

Basil

Bay leaf

Chives

Cilantro/coriander

Dill

Lemongrass

Marjoram

Mint

Oregano

Parsley

Rosemary

Sage

Tarragon

Thyme

HOW TO STORE FRESH HERBS

You can buy most fresh herbs in small pots and keep them on the countertop at room temperature. If, however, you're buying cut herbs, snip off the bottoms of the stems and put them in a jar with a little water, like a vase. Most herbs need to be refrigerated and should be kept away from too much air, which you can do by loosely covering them with a reusable bag or wrap on top of the jar or by storing them in a bigger jar and closing it with a lid. Some herbs, like basil, are best kept at room temperature, as cold temperatures can damage their texture. You can keep basil in a jar with a little water as well, but there's no need for a lid. Just make sure it's not exposed to direct sunlight.

BULB & STEM VEGETABLES

Asparagus

Celeriac

Celery

Fennel

Garlic

Kohlrabi

Leeks

Onions (green, white, or red)

NIGHTSHADES

Bell peppers

Eggplant

Okra

Tomatoes

Tomatillos

White potatoes

ROOT VEGETABLES

Beets

Burdock

Carrots

Jícama

Parsnips

Radishes

Sweet potatoes

Turnips

Yams

CRUCIFERAE (THE CABBAGE FAMILY) AND FLOWER BUDS

Artichokes

Bok choy

Broccoli

Broccolini

Brussels sprouts

Cabbage (white, purple)

Cauliflower

SQUASHES

Acorn

Butternut

Delicata

Hokkaido

Kabocha

Yellow summer squash

Zucchini

SEA VEGETABLES

Sea vegetables can give dishes a fish-like taste, which is why they're often used in mock tuna dishes or other vegan imitation seafoods.

Irish moss

Kelp

Nori

Seaweed

Wakame

HOW TO STORE FRESH PRODUCE

Store your vegetables (except for root vegetables) in the fridge. If you want your leafy greens to stay fresh longer, store them in biodegradable produce bags and remove as much air as possible. Bell peppers can be stored on the countertop or in the fridge. I prefer storing them at room temperature.

Most fruit should be kept outside the fridge so it can ripen properly and develop its full flavor. Here are a few specifics and exceptions:

Avocados Avocados do not like the cold, so make sure you store them at room temperature. If you're making guacamole and want to store it in the fridge without it turning brown, a trick is to add a thin layer of water on top and then pour it off once you take it out of the fridge. When you use only half of an avocado, try not to remove the pit from the half you're not using. That will help keep it from going bad too quickly.

Berries Berries should always be kept in the fridge in order to remain fresh for as long as possible. It's also best to not wrap them in plastic or paper, as they can get moldy quickly.

Citrus Oranges, lemons, limes, grapefruits, and other citrus fruits can be stored on the countertop or in the fridge. The latter will keep them fresh longer.

Papayas Leave papayas on the countertop until they're ripe and then start refrigerating them to keep them from going bad too fast.

Pineapple Pineapples should be stored outside the fridge. If you can, try to store them upside down. Have you ever noticed how the bottom part of a pineapple is much sweeter than the top part? If you store them upside down while ripening, the fruit sugars can distribute more evenly.

Tomatoes Store tomatoes at room temperature. Refrigerating them keeps them from ripening and changes their texture and taste. An exception to the rule are market-fresh tomatoes that were picked at peak ripeness. They will keep longer if stored in the fridge, especially during hot summer months.

HOW TO FREEZE PRODUCE

You can easily freeze fresh produce, significantly reducing food waste and ensuring you always have some on hand for smoothies and quick meals. Freeze fruit when it's at its ripest and vegetables when they're still fresh.

TO FREEZE FRUIT

Fruit can simply be cut into chunks and frozen in a ziplock bag or reusable container. Be sure you freeze fruits without their peel and pit.

Frozen bananas are great in smoothies or banana ice cream. Make sure they are at peak ripeness (spotty and sweet smelling) before freezing. Peel them and freeze them, whole, in a ziplock bag or reusable container. It's easier to measure them if they're still whole, and they are easy to break or cut once frozen.

Another great way to freeze produce is to juice it and then freeze it in ice cube trays or reusable and freezable bottles.

TO FREEZE VEGETABLES

Vegetables and legumes like beans, peas, broccoli, Brussels sprouts, carrots, asparagus, and cauliflower should be blanched before freezing. This prevents dull colors and off textures and flavors. To blanch them, submerge them in boiling water for a couple of minutes and then in ice water to stop the cooking. Dry them with a kitchen towel and place them on a tray lined with parchment paper. Freeze them for at least a few hours and then transfer them to a reusable container in the freezer (to take up less space). Leafy greens like chard, kale, and spinach don't necessarily have to be blanched, but doing so will help reduce the space needed in the freezer, so the choice is yours. Starchy vegetables like squash and potatoes do not need to be blanched before being frozen, but you may want to oven-roast them first, so that you only need to reheat them for a short amount of time before eating them.

LEGUMES

Lentils and beans should be a staple food in every vegan kitchen. They're an excellent source of plant-based protein, and they're filling, tasty, and easy to incorporate into savory dishes, salads, and even healthy desserts. They are available cooked and canned, or uncooked and dried; both kinds keep well for a long time. Store dried beans and legumes in a cool, dry place, but never in the refrigerator.

LENTILS

Black or beluga lentils

Brown lentils

French lentils

Green lentils

Red lentils

Split peas

Yellow lentils

BEANS

Adzuki beans

Black beans

Black-eyed peas

Butter beans

Cannellini beans

Chickpeas/garbanzo beans

Cranberry beans

Great northern beans

Kidney beans

Lima beans

Lupin beans

Mung beans

Navy beans

Pinto beans

Soybeans

SOY PRODUCTS

Edamame

Soybeans

Soy milk

Tempeh

Tofu

STARCHY VEGETABLES

Starchy vegetables are excellent staple foods, as they're very affordable, easy to digest, and filling. The best way to prepare them is by steaming, boiling, or roasting them. They're higher in calories than other vegetables such as leafy greens, making it easier to meet your caloric needs without having to eat enormous volumes. To give you an example, it would take approximately 255 cups of chopped kale but only 10 cups of boiled potatoes to consume 2,000 calories. Store starchy vegetables in a cool, well-ventilated place. They can be stored both outside the fridge and in the fridge.

Corn (also a grain)

Potatoes

Sweet potatoes

Winter squash

Yams

SOY
Why the
BAD REPUTATION?

First things first. Let's remember that soy is, after all, a bean. It's not a chemical or a toxin, it's a legume just like any other bean and populations all over the globe have been eating it for many, many generations. The reason soy in particular is often linked to misinformation and confusion is that it contains phyto-estrogen, the molecules of which are very similar in shape to the molecules of estrogen. That is why people believe that eating soy will affect their hormone levels in a negative way. Phytoestrogen, however, does not affect the body in the same way estrogen would. Generally speaking, unless you have an allergy or sensitivity, soy consumed in moderation (as edamame, tofu, tempeh, or soy milk, for instance) is absolutely fine.

GRAINS

Be sure to store your grains in airtight containers, such as glass or stainless steel containers, in a cool environment. Heat, moisture, and air all have adverse effects on grains.

Amaranth

Barley (contains gluten)

Buckwheat

Bulgur (contains gluten)

Corn

Couscous (contains gluten)

Farro (contains gluten)

Kamut (contains gluten)

Millet

Oats (**Note:** Oats are naturally gluten-free, but they're often processed in the same facilities as wheat products, so if you have celiac disease, avoid oats unless the package certifies they're gluten-free.)

Quinoa

Rice

Rye (contains gluten)

Sorghum

Spelt (contains gluten)

Wheat and wheat products like pasta and bread (contain gluten)

NUTS & SEEDS

Nuts and seeds are a great source of healthy fats and are extremely versatile. The difference between nuts and seeds is that nuts generally have a hard outer shell that has difficulty separating from the edible portion, which is why we use tools such as

nutcrackers. Seeds typically have an outer husk that is much easier to remove. However, not all seeds need the husk to be removed in order for them to be edible.

NUTS

Almonds

Brazil nuts

Chestnuts (**Note:** Chestnuts are larger nuts with an extremely hard shell that can be hard to open. They're also much lower in fat and higher in carbohydrates than other nuts and cause allergies less frequently.)

Hazelnuts

Pecans

Pine nuts

Pistachios

Walnuts

SEEDS

Chia seeds

Hemp seeds

Flaxseed

Poppy seeds

Pumpkin seeds

Sesame seeds

Sunflower seeds

Note: Peanuts are technically legumes, but they're often listed alongside nuts because of their higher fat content and crunchy texture, which make them more similar to nuts.

HOW TO STORE NUTS & SEEDS

While it's okay to store nuts and seeds at room temperature, they can go rancid quickly due to their high fat content. Light, heat, and oxygen can also make them go rancid. It's ideal to store them in airtight containers in the refrigerator or even the freezer, or another dark, cool place, especially when they've previously been ground or roasted.

OILS

Oils are fats that have been extracted from fruits, vegetables, nuts, or seeds. Whenever possible, it's preferable to eat fats in their original state. For example, it's better to eat the avocado than the avocado oil, the olives than the olive oil, etc. But there's no harm in including some oil in your diet, for cooking and sautéing vegetables, for instance.

A Word on GLUTEN

Most unprocessed foods, with the exception of some whole grains, are naturally gluten-free, which makes it very easy to adapt the 28-day reset to a gluten-free diet if you choose. Where bread or pasta is called for, choose gluten-free versions if appropriate for you. Unless you have an intolerance or allergy, however, abstaining from gluten is not a must.

COCONUT OIL: REFINED VS. UNREFINED

Unrefined coconut oil is extracted directly from a fresh coconut and maintains some of the coconut flavor. Refined coconut oil is extracted from dried coconut, which leaves it with much less, if any, coconut flavor.

Avocado oil

Canola oil

Coconut oil

Flaxseed oil

Olive oil

Peanut oil

Rapeseed oil

Walnut oil

HOW TO STORE OILS

Most oils can be stored at room temperature even after opening, but they should be sealed tightly and stored in a cool, dark place, never next to the stove. Store oil in the fridge if you don't use it often. Some oils, like flaxseed oil, go rancid quickly and need to be refrigerated at all times. You'll usually find these in opaque containers in the refrigerated section of the supermarket.

OTHER CONDIMENTS & SEASONINGS

An array of condiments and seasonings—such as vinegars, maple syrup, extracts, and spices—can add flavor and sometimes nutrients to your food. Here are a few notable ingredients:

Liquid smoke Adds a hint of barbecue flavor to vegetables, beans, or anything else you add it to, making it one of my favorite ingredients to use when veganizing traditionally non-vegan dishes.

Nutritional yeast This has a slightly cheesy and nutty taste to it and is also high in protein and B vitamins. You can add it to soups, dressings, salads, and pasta sauces.

Salt Try to avoid refined table salt, as it's been stripped of all its nutritional benefits. Opt for Himalayan pink salt or Celtic sea salt instead.

Pumpkin spice You can make your own pumpkin spice blend by mixing ground cinnamon, ground ginger, ground nutmeg, and ground cloves.

Kala namak This black salt is my secret weapon in the kitchen whenever I miss the taste of eggs. It contains sulfur, making it taste a lot like hard-boiled eggs. I love it on top of ripe avocados, with tofu as a vegan scramble, or with chickpeas, greens, and a little vegan mayo as a quick meal.

how to cook beans

If using canned beans, no preparation is needed. If starting with dried, soak the beans in cold water overnight or for at least 4 hours before cooking. Drain them, transfer to a large pot, and add water to cover by 2 inches. Simmer until tender; different beans have different cooking times, so read the package instructions. Let cool and then store in an airtight container in the refrigerator.

Notes:

1. *Soaking the beans will only reduce the cooking time by 10 to 15 minutes, so if you forget this step, no worries at all; simply cook them a bit longer.*
2. *If you have a pressure cooker, you can use it to cook the beans, which is quicker and requires no soaking.*

how to cook rice

Combine 1 part rice and 2 parts water (for example, 1 cup rice and 2 cups water, or scale up or down) in a pot. Bring to a boil. Reduce the heat to low and cook, covered, until the rice is tender. White rice will take 15 to 20 minutes; brown rice will take 30 to 45; wild rice will take 40 to 60. Turn off the heat and let the rice sit for 5 to 10 minutes, then fluff with a fork. One cup of dry rice will make 3 cups cooked.

how to cook quinoa

Combine 1 part quinoa and 2 parts water in a pot. Bring to a boil. Reduce the heat to low and cook, covered, until the quinoa has absorbed all of the water, about 15 minutes. Fluff with a fork. One cup of dry quinoa will make 3 cups cooked. Use this same method to cook millet.

soaking cashews (and other nuts and seeds)

Cashews are high in fat, which makes them a good base for creamy sauces. Soak them in water for at least 2 to 3 hours, or even better, overnight, before blending them, unless you are using a high-speed blender, in which case you can omit the soaking step. Follow these instructions for soaking other nuts or seeds as well.

GROCERY SHOPPING & MONEY-SAVING TIPS

Adopting a new diet and lifestyle also means adapting to a new way to shop and spend money. Veganism is often associated with overall higher costs and products that are difficult to find. Many processed alternatives to meat, cheese, and eggs tend to indeed be on the pricier side, leaving the impression that veganism is something not everyone can afford. Furthermore, many vegan companies producing alternatives to meat, dairy, and eggs also invest in quality, fair wages, and eco-conscious practices, which adds to the cost. Animal agriculture is heavily subsidized by the government, making meat and dairy less expensive, while fresh produce and other plant-based foods only receive a very small fraction of these subsidies. The good news is that a plant-based diet based on whole foods including legumes, grains, and starches instead of processed foods can be very affordable. Here are a few tips to help you save money.

Choose legumes over processed foods Beans, peas, and lentils are very high in fiber and protein, are healthy and sustainable, and are affordable.

Buy in bulk Buying in bulk is one of the best things you can do to save money, and most grocery stores have bulk bins for dried goods like beans and nuts. Since no packaging is involved, this is also a much more eco-friendly option: Bring your own reusable bags and containers to the store and then transfer the bulk foods to glass containers and jars at home.

Compare prices Take note of prices at different stores and compare them. It may not always be convenient to do your grocery shopping at multiple stores, but being aware of the prices can help you plan your shopping trips accordingly. Even within one store, compare prices of different staple foods.

Shop at farmers' markets If you have a farmers' market in your neighborhood, get to know the farmers. If you go regularly, they'll start recognizing you and may even give you the occasional extra discount. Going to the market right before it closes can also save you money, since the farmers will often rather sell the rest of their produce at a cheaper price than have to take it back with them and risk not selling it at all.

Shop at wholesale markets This is a good alternative for larger families or people who share their groceries with roommates. Wholesale markets are where many stores buy their produce. They usually look like big market halls and fruits and vegetables are sold by the case well below retail price. You may not be able to find one in your immediate vicinity, but often the prices are so low that it's worth a special trip.

Prioritize local and seasonal foods Fruits and vegetables can be up to three or even four times more expensive when they're not in season. Buy produce that's in season and that's produced locally.

It doesn't always have to be organic Organic doesn't always mean better. Not all organic produce is pesticide-free, and not all conventionally grown produce is sprayed with pesticides. Many farmers grow produce using sustainable, fair-trade practices but don't opt for organic certification. Often, imported organic fruits and vegetables also have a much larger ecological footprint and have to be picked long before they're ripe, making them less nutrient-dense.

Plan The meal plans in this book are designed to be economical, since you will use the same ingredients for several meals, decreasing waste and lowering the risk of overbuying food. If you know that you'll be out and about most of the day and don't want to spend money on buying meals or snacks, pack your own. Nuts, seeds, and fruits like apples are easy to transport and don't require refrigeration.

Opt for generic brands Many stores carry their own brand, which they sell at a lower price than well-known national brands.

Make more frequent trips to the supermarket It's easy to overestimate the amount of food you'll need, especially when it comes to fresh produce like leafy greens. If you live near a supermarket or farmers' market, try to stick with smaller quantities so you don't overbuy.

Freeze food If you do end up with more fresh produce than you need, freezing it is a great way to make sure it doesn't go to waste. See page 26 for tips.

Opt for frozen or canned food if there's a significant price difference Frozen food or cans and jars can be more affordable than fresh produce, and also more convenient when you need to prepare a quick meal. I still think fresh produce is better, but frozen and canned produce are the next best option. Look for recyclable glass jars and BPA-free cans, if you can.

Shop online Many online shops, some of which are subscription-based, like Thrive Market, offer great discounts on nonperishable items, often saving you about 20 to 50 percent compared to retail prices.

Prioritize Last, but not least, an investment in the food you eat is an investment in your health and well-being. Take a look at everything else you're currently spending money on—for example, electronics, cosmetics, or clothes—and evaluate where food fits into that picture.

You can have the healthiest diet and still be unhappy or feel imbalanced. That's because our lives and our well-being revolve around and depend on so much more than just the food we eat. How we move and breathe, how much rest we get, how we talk to ourselves, and who we surround ourselves with is just as important, which is why we need to pay attention to and take care of all parts of ourselves. I encourage you to embrace a holistic lifestyle, which means one that addresses the whole system rather than only part.

Move

Moving your body on a regular basis, ideally every day, is essential to feeling good. Staying active can help lower the risk of heart disease, diabetes, strokes, high blood pressure, and many other health issues. It can also help reduce stress and improve overall sleep quality. While exercise can undoubtedly help you get and stay in shape, you'll enjoy it much more if you focus on feeling good now and doing it because it's fun and it brings you joy.

"'i love myself.'
the
quietest.
simplest.
most
powerful.
revolution.
ever."
—Nayyirah Waheed

Do the best you can

I can't stress this enough, but don't be too hard on yourself. Push yourself beyond what feels comfortable, but also focus on small victories. Be both optimistic and realistic when it comes to your fitness goals. That means that you should set goals that are beyond what you ever thought possible, but also accept that it may take some time to get there. If you never work out and your goal is to run a marathon, fantastic! But keep in mind that it will take many smaller steps in order to get there, and try to celebrate

every single one of them. It really is just as much about the journey as it is about the end result. Be your own cheerleader and support system. So often, we end up being harder on ourselves than anyone else could ever be. I know this all too well, because I've dealt with this for most of my life. We focus on our shortcomings and the things we lack, often becoming our own worst enemies. If you notice yourself thinking negative thoughts about yourself and the progress you're making or think you're not making, try to gently catch yourself and shift the negative words to more encouraging ones. Instead of thinking, "I'll never get there," try, "I'm proud of every step and I'll just keep getting better." We're often afraid of what others may think or say about us, but the truth is that they think about us so much more rarely than we imagine and often not at all. Most people are too busy thinking about themselves and their own insecurities to think about ours.

Breathe

Breathing helps us detoxify and cleanse our bodies and at the same time regulates stress levels. Proper breathing is incredibly important for our overall well-being, yet we tend to under-breathe, meaning that while we breathe more quickly, we don't breathe deeply enough. How many times a minute do you breathe in and out? How deep are the breaths you take? We are often so busy and stressed that we don't pay attention to our breath and therefore become quick and shallow breathers. You may be so used to feeling stressed that you don't even realize that you are stressed anymore.

Our breath is closely linked to our thoughts and emotions, and breathing deeply can have an immediate effect on how you feel when you're under emotional distress. Have you ever noticed your breath or body temperature changing as you got upset about something? Everything is connected, and so by learning to control your breath, you can learn to influence your emotions as well. Here are a few basic breathing techniques that you can practice daily:

DEEP BREATHING

1. Close your eyes and sit or lie in a comfortable position. If you're sitting, make sure your back is straight and your shoulders are relaxed.

2. Exhale all the air that is still in your lungs. Breathe out in an almost exaggerated way.

3. Take a deep and long breath in for a count of 4 and then an even deeper breath out for a count of 8.

4. Repeat this for 10 to 15 breaths and try to see if you can make your breaths even longer as you proceed.

Sometimes focusing on a specific mantra, like "om," or a short positive affirmation can help you focus even more. If you're having a hard time finding positive affirmations, try taking one of your biggest fears or concerns and making your affirmation the opposite of that. So, if you're constantly stressed or don't think you are doing well enough at work or school, try a phrase like "I do my best and trust the rest." You can think "I do my best" when you breathe in and "and trust the rest" when you breathe out. The beauty of this is that you don't have to believe what you're saying—that's kind of the point. You say what you wish you believed, and if you repeat it often enough, you'll eventually start believing it, too.

THREE-PART BREATHING

1. Sit in a comfortable position or lie on your back with your legs bent, which will help relax your psoas.

2. Exhale all the air that is still in your lungs through your nose.

3. Place your hands on your upper rib cage on each side and breathe into that part of your body for a count of 4 (which means that you intentionally don't make your breaths as deep). Breathe out for a count of 6 to 8.

4. Repeat 10 times.

5. Now lower your hands to right below your rib cage and breathe into that part (a little deeper). In for a count of 4, out for a count of 6 to 8. Repeat 10 times.

6. Lower your hands all the way to your lower stomach and now breathe all the way into your stomach (very deep breaths). In for a count of 4, out for a count of 6 to 8. Repeat 10 times.

Restore

This technique is ideal at the end of a long day or if you just feel like you want to let go of something (or someone).

1. Stand with your feet a little wider than hip distance apart and soften your knees.

2. Pull your shoulders up to your ears and then let them fall. Repeat this a few times until you feel a little more relaxed.

3. Let your arms hang loose and make sure your back is straight.

4. Take a deep breath in and, right before you exhale, focus on everything you want to let go—your stress, your problems, everything. Visualize it right in front of you.

5. As you exhale, let your whole upper body fall to the front (as if you were a puppet hanging from a string and someone let go of the strings controlling the upper body). Sigh loudly as you exhale all the air from your lungs and imagine that everything you want to let go of is just falling from your body and drifting away.

6. Repeat as many times as you wish!

> *"And the day came when the risk to remain tight in a bud was more painful than the risk it took to blossom."*
> —Anaïs Nin, writer

SLEEP

Your body needs the rest it gets while it's asleep to heal and recover. Getting less sleep than you actually need can result in an overall lack of energy and put you at risk for numerous health issues. According to the American Academy of Sleep Medicine, about one in five adults fail to get enough sleep. Sleep deprivation (less than seven hours of sleep per night) increases the risk of excessive daytime sleepiness, changes in mood (including irritability, lack of motivation, anxiety, and depression), lack of concentration, fatigue, and even high blood pressure, heart attacks, and obesity.

Getting enough sleep is crucial, but it's not just the amount of sleep that is important; the quality of sleep matters, too. If you think you're getting enough sleep but you still don't feel rested or refreshed when you wake up in the morning, here are some things you can try:

Avoid stimulants like caffeine and other substances that interfere with sleep quality (including alcohol and nicotine) in the hours before going to bed.

Create your ideal sleeping environment. Make sure the temperature is just right (60° to 75°F, or 15° to 23°C, feels best for most people) and that the room is well ventilated. If you're sensitive to light, try using heavy curtains or an eye mask.

Go to sleep when you're tired. Sounds easy enough, but how many of us have struggled to close our eyes while already lying in bed? If you've been in bed for more than 30 minutes and just can't fall asleep, get up and listen to soothing music or do some stretches until you are tired enough to sleep.

Create your very own pre-bedtime routine. Your bedtime routine should consist of anything that relaxes you, which could include restorative yoga, meditation, breathing exercises, or listening to music.

Leave the day (and your worries) behind. Something that has helped me personally is journaling at the end of the day or making a list of everything I need to do or that worries me in any way. This does two things: 1) It takes it out of your mind and onto the paper (or screen); and 2) It shows you that your worries are manageable and not that overwhelming. If you go to bed with a clear idea of what needs to be done the next day, you'll be more relaxed and sleep better.

If you're someone who has to get up very early (when it's still dark out), **consider investing in a dawn simulator alarm clock.** It slowly and gently starts emitting light and you will naturally wake up a couple of minutes before the alarm even rings. If you want to find out more about the effect light has on sleep quality, I'd recommend reading the book *The Instinct to Heal* by David Servan-Schreiber.

Sleep in or nap whenever you can. Instead of taking a 30-minute coffee break, why not try to take a power nap instead?

Have early dinners so you don't feel too heavy when you go to bed. Luckily, vegan food digests much more easily and quickly than animal products, so even if you do have late dinners, it won't affect you quite as much.

Exercise! Daily exercise, even just fifteen to thirty minutes, will contribute to your overall well-being, but make sure you don't do it too close to your bedtime, since you may feel a little agitated afterward.

Stay hydrated—with just the right amount. Drink enough water before bedtime that you won't wake up thirsty in the middle of the night, but not so much that you'll have to get up every hour to use the bathroom.

THE DIFFERENCE BETWEEN REST & SLEEP

There is a difference between rest and sleep. Have you ever woken up after sleeping for ten hours straight, yet somehow you still felt exhausted? Even sleep can be exhausting when you're trying to process everything that happened while you were awake. You may have very active dreams or you might be moving around all night. If that is the case for you, I would suggest trying meditation. When practiced regularly, meditation can give you more rest than sleep does. An hour of meditation can be as beneficial as four hours of deep sleep.

MEDITATION

Meditation isn't just for those who have trouble sleeping. It can significantly reduce your stress levels and make you feel happier and more relaxed. The core idea of mediation is to calm your mind and your thoughts so as to reconnect with and center yourself. Here are some tips on how to get started:

Find a seated position that feels comfortable to you. Sit up straight in whatever way you think you'll be able to sit without moving too much for a few minutes. This may be a cross-legged position, sitting with your legs stretched out, or sitting on a chair.

Meditate first thing in the morning. Any time is a good time to meditate, but the morning hours right after waking up are ideal. Your mind won't be as full from the worries of the day and you'll be likely to have an easier time relaxing and letting go.

Start small. Meditating sounds a lot easier than it is. We're so used to being distracted all day every day that sitting quietly can seem challenging. Start with just five minutes a day and then slowly work your way up to fifteen to twenty minutes. If you think you don't have time to meditate, remember this Zen proverb: *"You should sit in meditation for twenty minutes every day—unless you're too busy. Then you should sit for an hour."*

Don't try not to think. If I told you not to think of a big red balloon, what you would you immediately think of? Probably a big red balloon. Thoughts are inevitable. Instead, try to observe them and then let them go without engaging with them.

Focus on something. One of the best ways to start meditating is to focus all of your attention on one thing. You can light a candle and focus on the flame until you feel the need to close your eyes. You'll still see the light flickering in your mind and can keep focusing on it. Quiet and repetitive sounds like the sound of the air-conditioning and/or your breath are excellent things to focus on as well. If you feel too many thoughts coming in while you're focusing on your breath, try quietly thinking the word "in" each time you breathe in and "out" each time you breathe out.

Try guided meditations. These are excellent for beginners and those who have particularly restless minds. You'll find them in written form or as podcasts or audio tracks. Here is one short guided meditation you can use whenever you feel stressed or overwhelmed by negative emotions or thoughts.

....
**VISUALIZATION BREATH:
A MINI GUIDED MEDITATION**

1. Lie down on your back in a comfortable position either on the floor or on your bed. Feel free to play some classical or other relaxing music in the background, but just make sure it's not too loud and that it will help you relax more deeply. Your feet should be about hip distance apart or a little wider. Take a mental tour of your body and check if all the parts of your body are relaxed. If any part feels tense, tighten the muscles in that area even more and then let go completely.

2. Close your eyes and start taking deep breaths. As you exhale, try to visualize any negative emotions or stress factors in your body as a dark gray mass. Let your imagination decide on the texture and exact look; it could be smoke-like or a gooey substance. Associate that

gray mass with all the negative things in your life you'd like to let go of—everything that's making you feel heavy, like fears, worries, guilt, shame. As your breath fully exits your lungs, imagine something pulling that mass out of you and visualize it leaving your body.

3. As you inhale, imagine a golden white and warm light slowly entering your body and filling every cell of your body with more light. Associate that light with everything you feel grateful for and everything that brings you joy, such as a loved one, a song you like, sunshine, anything. As you inhale and exhale, visualize the gray mass leaving your body entirely until you are filled with only the light and you feel an overall sense of warmth and well-being.

4. Repeat this for at least ten breaths or for as long as you wish. You can do this at any time of the day and as often as you wish.

....
JOURNALING

You'll find a few journaling questions at the beginning and the end of each week of the meal plan. This part of the Vegan Reset is optional, but highly recommended. Feel free to use the questions as guidelines only or to come up with your own questions. Self-reflection can be a very useful tool when you're changing your eating habits.

Self-love & self-care

Emotional health and mental health are just as important as physical health. They affect your relationships, your overall well-being, and everything else in your life and therefore should be a priority.

Putting yourself first is anything but selfish. All too often we're taught to take care of everyone else, but we don't always extend that kindness to ourselves. Self-care is about identifying your own needs and then making sure they are met so that you don't burn out. This can mean allowing yourself to take a nap or a bath when you feel tired and overworked, going for a walk, treating yourself to a massage, or listening to music. We may feel like other things are more important, but if we neglect to take care of ourselves, we will feel the consequences sooner or later.

Loving and accepting yourself is so much easier said than done and so much more important than we could possibly imagine. The relationship you have with yourself sets the tone for every other relationship in your life. The truth is, when you're used to being self-critical, showing yourself kindness can seem like the most challenging thing in the world. People often say that in order to change, you have to first accept and love yourself fully, just the way you are. Before I understood the true meaning of this concept, it always seemed absurd to me. I felt that if I loved and accepted myself the way I was, I wouldn't feel the need to change. Accepting yourself the way you are is about realizing that you are worthy no matter what you look or feel like or what anyone says. Worthiness has no prerequisites. Learning the value of that is a process, and it starts with making the decision to be a little kinder to yourself and then making that decision again and again, every single day. It means forgiving yourself when you forget to be patient, it means giving yourself as many second chances as you need.

Healing old wounds

Weight issues and other forms of self-sabotage are often the result of emotional wounds that have been left unattended. By ignoring them, you allow the past to hurt you over and over again in the present. These wounds can be the result of someone making you doubt yourself when you were child, a parent who treated you unkindly, or any traumatic event. Every time someone told me that I was strange, that I

wasn't good enough, that I was too big, too weird, too different, too fat, it left its mark on me, and I ended up believing all the things they said. Not only that, I started saying them to myself as well. I started using food to numb not just the negative emotions, but all emotions. But by doing that, I never really allowed those emotional wounds to heal—instead, they stayed with me for years.

Things only started getting better when I finally realized that being numb was more unbearable than the actual pain. I started paying close attention to the moments in which I felt like overeating, smoking, or drinking. Identifying those moments then allowed me to find different ways to handle them. It took many attempts to get to a better place, and I'd be lying if I said that I didn't still have moments of self-doubt, but with time, it got better and better even though I once truly believed it never would.

When I finally allowed myself to grieve my father's death, the sadness was so painful that I sometimes didn't know if I'd be able to handle it. Once you truly let yourself feel whatever it is you've been trying not to feel, once you accept that there is no easy way out, you can let go of the resistance and stop being your own worst enemy, one step at a time.

Most of us are works in progress and will probably always be. Life is not about reaching an end point where everything is perfect; it's about finding, creating, and celebrating yourself every step of the way. The 28-day program in this book includes daily reminders and exercises that will help guide you on this journey. No matter where you're at right now, remember that you are not alone and that the past does not have to determine the future. Every new day is a new opportunity to be a little kinder to yourself and to regain control of your own happiness.

Part

TWO

The 28-Day Program

Journaling Exercise

Back to the future exercise Take a notepad and write a letter to your future self about what you hope to accomplish, how you hope to feel, and what you wish to improve over the next four weeks. Seal the letter and keep it sealed until the end of the program.

Exercise & Meditation During the Vegan Reset

Daily: Every day, walk, dance, or choose a different kind of activity for at least 30 minutes.

Weekly: If you can, add another form of exercise like a yoga, Pilates, or group fitness class, three times a week.

Daily meditation practice If you're new to meditating, begin with 5 minutes a day, ideally first thing in the morning, and then increase the practice by another 5 minutes every week. See page 35 for more information on meditation and a sample guided meditation.

> WEEK 1: 5 minutes of meditation a day
>
> WEEK 2: 10 minutes of meditation a day
>
> WEEK 3: 15 minutes of meditation a day
>
> WEEK 4: 20 minutes of meditation a day

Daily Journaling Practice

Every morning, write down five things that you are grateful for. These things can be people, belongings, actions, elements, or anything that comes to mind and that you feel grateful for.

If You Have
ALLERGIES

Tree nuts Use seeds like sunflower or pumpkin seeds instead of nuts. Use sunflower seed butter, hemp seeds, or ground flax seed instead of peanut butter, and instead of nut milk, use soy, hemp, or oat milk.

Soy Omit the soy sauce/tamari or use balsamic vinegar instead. Use any legumes like white beans or chickpeas instead of tofu and tempeh.

Gluten Use gluten-free bread and noodles. Soy sauce can contain gluten, so omit it or look for tamari that is clearly labeled gluten-free.

Important Notes for the Weekly Shopping Lists and Meal Plans

1. All items that are in italics are staple foods that you'll use during the other weeks as well. If your grocery store sells some of them in bulk (like beans or nuts), you can buy exactly the amount you'll need each week, or buy more than you need and keep them stocked in your pantry.

2. Even if you will be able to use some staple ingredients beyond the first weeks, I understand that many people are on a tight budget and won't want to buy every ingredient or seasoning at once. Every item with a * next to it is optional in order to make the list more budget friendly.

3. This meal plan can be gluten-free if you have an allergy or intolerance. You can opt for regular or gluten-free bread and pasta. Just make sure they're egg-, dairy-, and honey-free.

A Note About Calories

Each day contains approximately 2,000 calories, which is the standard recommendation for women. The weekly meal plans are meant as a guide, but you do not need to follow them strictly. Feel free to adjust the plans as you see fit. You may need slightly fewer calories or significantly more depending on your height, gender, and activity level. You can use an online calorie counter to find out how many calories you need each day.

A Note on COFFEE

Caffeine is a stimulant, so it's best consumed in moderation, but definitely okay to enjoy occasionally. Make sure the coffee you purchase comes from a company that supports fair trade, ethical working conditions, and sustainable practices. I generally recommend that people try to either limit their caffeine intake or avoid caffeine altogether during the 28-day reset. The main reason for that is so that you can observe how your body responds in different situations and you can identity your needs better. We often rely on coffee to keep us awake and focused when what we really need is more rest, more water, or more nutrient-dense food.

"Acknowledging the good that you already have in your life is the foundation for all abundance."
—*Eckhart Tolle*

Week One
SHOPPING LIST

FRUITS

Bananas	11
Lemons	6
Fresh mango	1
Watermelon	1
Pears	6
Oranges	2
Lime	1
Medjool dates	3
Fresh berries* (of your choice)	1 pint
Apples	3
Blackberries*	1 pint
Dried cranberries, unsweetened	1 package
Frozen raspberries	1 package
Frozen mango	1 package

VEGETABLES

Sweet potatoes	4
Green onions	1 bunch
Garlic	1 bulb
Onion	1
Zucchini	2
Bell peppers	4
Brussels sprouts	6 ounces (about 1 cup)
Celery	1 head
Carrots	1 bag or bunch
Romaine lettuce	1 head
Purple cabbage	1 small head
Cucumber	1
Yellow potatoes	4
Cauliflower	1 head
Kale	1 large or 2 small packages (10 cups)
Broccoli	1 head
Cherry tomatoes	1 pint
Corn kernels	two 15-ounce cans (or use frozen corn)
Tomato*	1
Avocados	5
Green beans	5 ounces
Portobello mushroom	1

FRESH HERBS

Cilantro	1 bunch or package

LEGUMES

Chickpeas	two 15-ounce cans or 8 ounces (1 cup) dried
Extra-firm tofu	one 8-ounce package
Black beans	two 15-ounce cans or 8 ounces (1 cup) dried

NUTS & SEEDS

Peanuts*	2 ounces (about ⅓ cup)
Pumpkin seeds*	1 ounce
Ground flaxseed	1 ounce
Almonds*	1 ounce
Cashews	10 ounces
Sunflower seeds	1.5 ounces

GRAINS

Brown rice	7 ounces (1 cup)
Soft corn tortillas or frozen or hard taco shells	1 package
Rice noodles	1 package
Oats	1 container (any size; you will need ½ cup)

MYLK

Unsweetened almond milk	1 quart

CONDIMENTS & STAPLE FOODS

Maple syrup	Vanilla extract*
Olive oil	Liquid smoke*
Tahini*	Peanut butter
Apple cider vinegar*	Tamari or soy sauce
Sea salt	Smoked paprika*
Balsamic vinegar	Cornstarch*
Vegetable broth*	Mustard
Nutritional yeast*	Curry powder
Ground black pepper	Crushed red pepper flakes*

DAY 1

Breakfast Raspberry–Peanut Butter Shake

Lunch Purple Cabbage Boats with Peanut Tofu

Snack Watermelon & Pear

Dinner Loaded Sweet Potatoes

DAY 2

Breakfast Watermelon & Orange Slices

Lunch Sweet Potato Bowl

Snack Fruit & Peanut Butter

Dinner Chickpea Cabbage Boats

DAY 3

Breakfast Pink & Orange Layered Smoothie

Lunch Chickpea Tacos

Snack Veggies & Tahini

Dinner Corn & Tomato Soup

DAY 4

Breakfast Pears & Cream

Lunch Corn-Avocado Tacos

Snack Fruit

Dinner Rice Noodles with Veggies & Peanut Sauce

DAY 5

Breakfast Overnight Oats

Lunch Potato-Veggie Bowl

Snack Fruit

Dinner Green Bean Plate with Potato-Cauliflower Mash

DAY 6

Breakfast Savory Breakfast Bowl

Lunch Portobello Mushroom Bowl

Snack Fruit & Peanut Butter

Dinner Stuffed Bell Pepper

DAY 7

Breakfast Jumbo Green Smoothie

Lunch Black Bean Tacos

Snack Fruit & Nuts

Dinner Kale-Lemon Salad

Week One

MENU

Day
0 MEAL PREP

Cook the Chickpeas (if using dried)

You will need 2 cups cooked chickpeas. If using canned beans, you'll need 2 cans, no preparation needed. If starting with dried, cook 1 cup chickpeas as described on page 29. Let cool and then store in an airtight container in the refrigerator.

Prepare the Baked Sweet Potatoes

Halve 4 small sweet potatoes and bake at 400°F/200°C for 45 minutes. Let cool and store in an airtight container in the fridge.

Freeze the Bananas

Place 3 peeled bananas in a ziplock bag (or reusable container) in the freezer.

Make the Peanut Tofu

Makes 2 servings

8 ounces extra-firm tofu
1 green onion, chopped
1 garlic clove, minced
1 tablespoon olive oil
¼ cup peanuts, chopped
2 tablespoons peanut butter
1 tablespoon tamari or soy sauce
½ teaspoon smoked paprika
Pinch of sea salt

1. Remove any excess liquid from the tofu (using a kitchen towel), then cut into ½-inch cubes.

2. Sauté the green onion and garlic in the oil over high heat for 2 minutes.

3. Reduce the heat to medium and add the peanuts, peanut butter, soy sauce, paprika, and salt, mixing well. Add the tofu last. Cook for another 5 minutes.

4. Let cool and store in an airtight container in the fridge.

Make the Cooked Veggie Mix

Makes 4 servings

1 large onion, chopped
2 garlic cloves, minced
2 tablespoons olive oil
1 zucchini, diced
1 bell pepper, diced
1 cup Brussels sprouts, halved
2 celery stalks, chopped
2 carrots, chopped
2 green onions, chopped
½ teaspoon sea salt
Pinch of ground black pepper

1. Sauté the onion and garlic in the oil in a large pan or pot over medium to high heat for 2 minutes.

2. Add all of the remaining ingredients and cook for another 7 minutes.

3. Let cool and store in an airtight container in the fridge.

Prepare the Raw Veggie Mix

Makes 3 servings

2 stalks celery, finely chopped
1 bell pepper, diced, sliced, or chopped
1 head romaine lettuce, chopped
3 green onions, chopped
½ cup chopped purple cabbage (from about ¼ head)
½ small (or ¼ large) cucumber, chopped (optional)

1. Combine all of the ingredients and store in an airtight container in the fridge.

Cooked Veggie Mix

BAKED SWEET POTATOES

RAW VEGGIE MIX

PEANUT TOFU

CHICKPEAS

FROZEN BANANAS

Day 1

"We have to dare to be ourselves, however frightening or strange that self may prove to be."

—May Sarton, poet and novelist

BREAKFAST

Raspberry–Peanut Butter Shake

526 calories

Prep time: 2 minutes

Total time: 2 minutes

2 bananas
1 cup frozen raspberries
¾ cup almond milk
2 tablespoons peanut butter

1. Blend all of the ingredients in a blender until smooth. Enjoy!

LUNCH

Purple Cabbage Boats with Peanut Tofu

404 calories

Prep time: 2 minutes

Total time: 2 minutes (add 2 to 3 minutes if you choose to reheat the veggie mix and tofu)

2 purple cabbage leaves
1 serving Peanut Tofu (page 44)
1 serving Cooked Veggie Mix (page 44)
Fresh cilantro, for garnish (optional)

1. Fill the cabbage leaves with the tofu and the veggie mix.

2. Top with fresh cilantro, if using, and enjoy!

DINNER

Loaded Sweet Potatoes

605 calories

Prep time: 3 minutes

Total time: 3 minutes (add 2 to 3 minutes if you choose to reheat the sweet potatoes and veggie mix)

Sweet Potatoes

2 Baked Sweet Potatoes (page 44; 4 halves) insides slightly carved out and reserved
1 serving Cooked Veggie Mix (page 44)
Dash of ground black pepper

Sauce

The insides of the carved-out sweet potatoes (above)
⅓ cup cashews, soaked in water (see page 29)
Juice of 1 lemon
1 tablespoon nutritional yeast
1 teaspoon smoked paprika
Pinch of sea salt
1 teaspoon mustard
¼ cup almond milk

1. Fill the sweet potatoes with the veggie mix and sprinkle with the pepper.

2. Blend the sauce ingredients together in a blender until they reach a smooth consistency.

3. Top the sweet potatoes with the sauce, then enjoy!

SNACK

Fruit

402 calories

4 watermelon slices
1 pear

Raspberry–Peanut
Butter Shake

PURPLE CABBAGE
BOATS WITH
PEANUT TOFU

WATERMELON SLICES

PEAR

LOADED SWEET POTATOES

Day 2

"Don't take anything personally. Nothing others do is because of you. What others say and do is a projection of their own reality, their own dream. When you are immune to the opinions and actions of others, you won't be the victim of needless suffering."

—Miguel Ángel Ruiz, author of The Four Agreements

BREAKFAST

Watermelon & Orange Slices

473 calories

Prep time: 2 minutes
Total time: 2 minutes

¼ watermelon, sliced
2 oranges (cut into quarters)

SNACK

Fruit & Peanut Butter

403 calories

2 bananas
2 tablespoons peanut butter

LUNCH

Sweet Potato Bowl

549 calories

Prep time: 2 minutes
Total time: 2 minutes

2 Baked Sweet Potatoes (page 44;
    4 halves) diced
1 serving Peanut Tofu (page 44)
1 serving Raw Veggie Mix
    (page 44)

1. Combine all of the ingredients in a bowl and enjoy!

DINNER

Chickpea Cabbage Boats

550 calories

Prep time: 2 minutes
Cook time: 3 minutes
Total time: 5 minutes

Cabbage Boats
1 cup Cooked Chickpeas
    (see page 29)
1 tablespoon olive oil
1 teaspoon curry powder or
    ground turmeric
1 serving Cooked Veggie Mix
    (page 44)
2 purple cabbage leaves
Herbs of choice, for garnish
    (optional)

Maple Mustard
2 tablespoons mustard
1 tablespoon maple syrup

1. Cook the chickpeas with the olive oil and curry powder in a large skillet over high heat for 2 minutes.

2. Add the veggie mix to the pan and cook for another minute.

3. Mix the mustard and maple syrup with a fork or whisk.

4. Fill the cabbage leaves with the chickpea-veggie mixture, top with the maple mustard, garnish with herbs, if using, and enjoy!

WATERMELON
& ORANGE SLICES

SWEET POTATO BOWL

CHICKPEA
CABBAGE BOATS

Bananas & Peanut
Butter

Day

1,963 CALORIES
....

*"Your task is not to seek for love,
but merely to seek and find all
the barriers within yourself that
you have built against it."*

—Rumi, Persian poet

SNACK

Veggies & Tahini

370 calories

2 tablespoons tahini

Juice of 1 lemon

2 tablespoons water

Dash of sea salt

2 carrots, sliced

2 celery stalks

3 tablespoons almonds

1. Mix the tahini with the lemon
juice, water, and salt. Dip veggies
in the tahini mixture and enjoy
with the almonds.

BREAKFAST

Pink & Orange Layered Smoothie

544 calories

Prep time: 5 minutes

Total time: 5 minutes

Orange Layer
1 banana
1 cup frozen mango chunks
½ cup almond milk
1 tablespoon ground flaxseed

Pink Layer
1 banana
¾ cup frozen raspberries
½ cup almond milk
1 tablespoon ground flaxseed

1. Blend the ingredients for each
layer separately until smooth.
Layer in a mason jar or cup. Enjoy!

Note: You can blend all the ingredients
at once, for one uniform smoothie, to
save approximately 3 minutes on the
prep time.

LUNCH

Chickpea Tacos

540 calories

Prep time: 2 minutes

Total time: 2 minutes (add 2 to 3 minutes if
you choose to reheat the chickpeas)

3 soft corn tortillas

**1 cup Cooked Chickpeas
(page 29)**

**1 serving Raw Veggie Mix
(page 44)**

**⅓ cup cherry or grape tomatoes,
halved**

Juice of 1 lime

Pinch of sea salt

**Fresh herbs of choice, for garnish
(optional)**

1. Fill the tortillas with the
chickpeas, veggie mix, and
tomatoes. Top with the lime juice,
salt, and herbs, if using. Enjoy!

DINNER

Corn & Tomato Soup

509 calories

Prep time: 2 minutes

Cook time: 5 minutes

Total time: 7 minutes

**1 serving Cooked Veggie Mix
(page 44)**

1 cup corn kernels

⅔ cup diced tomatoes

**½ cup veggie broth, or ½ cup
water mixed with ½ teaspoon
veggie bouillon paste**

Sea salt and ground black pepper

1 avocado, diced

**Fresh herbs of choice, for garnish
(optional)**

1 teaspoon olive oil

1. Cook the veggie mix, corn,
tomatoes, and broth in a pot
over medium to high heat for
5 minutes. Transfer to a bowl.
Season with salt and pepper.

2. Top the soup with the avocado,
herbs, and a drizzle of olive oil.

WEEK
1

PINK & ORANGE
LAYERED SMOOTHIE

CHICKPEA
TACOS

Veggies & Tahini

CORN & TOMATO SOUP

Day 4

"So many people will tell you 'no,' and you need to find something you believe in so hard that you just smile and tell them 'watch me.' Learn to take rejection as motivation to prove people wrong. Be unstoppable. Refuse to give up, no matter what. It's the best skill you can ever learn."

—Charlotte Eriksson, Swedish songwriter and recording artist

BREAKFAST

Pears & Cream

549 calories

Prep time: 3 minutes

Total time: 3 minutes

Cashew Cream
⅓ cup cashews, soaked in water (see page 29)
Juice of 1 lemon
½ tablespoon water
½ teaspoon vanilla extract
4 pitted Medjool dates (or 1 tablespoon maple syrup)

Pears
2 sliced pears
2 teaspoons maple syrup

1. Blend all the cashew cream ingredients in a blender until smooth.

2. Combine the cashew cream with the pears, drizzle with maple syrup, and enjoy!

Fruit

179 calories

1 cup fresh berries
1 apple

LUNCH

Corn-Avocado Tacos

559 calories

Prep time: 3 minutes

Total time: 3 minutes

Dressing
½ avocado
Juice of 1 lemon
Pinch of sea salt
2 teaspoons olive oil

Tacos
3 soft corn tortillas
1 cup corn kernels
1 serving Raw Veggie Mix (page 44)

1. Mix or blend all of the dressing ingredients until they reach a smooth consistency.

2. Fill the tortillas with the corn, veggie mix, and dressing, and enjoy!

DINNER

Rice Noodles with Veggies & Peanut Sauce

686 calories

Prep time: 2 minutes

Cook time: 7 minutes

Total time: 9 minutes

Noodles & Veggies
3 ounces dried rice pasta
½ cup shredded purple cabbage
1 small (or ½ large) carrot, shredded (or very thinly sliced)
1 green onion, chopped
1 garlic clove, minced
2 teaspoons olive oil
1 tablespoon chopped peanuts
Fresh cilantro, for garnish

Sauce
2 tablespoons peanut butter
1 tablespoon tamari or soy sauce
1 tablespoon water
Pinch of sea salt
Pinch of crushed red pepper flakes (optional)

1. Cook the pasta according to the package instructions (3 to 7 minutes, depending on the brand).

2. Meanwhile, sauté the cabbage, carrot, green onion, and garlic in the oil in a pan over medium to high heat for 5 to 7 minutes.

3. Once the noodles are ready, add them to the pan with the veggies and mix well.

4. Mix all of the sauce ingredients using a fork or whisk.

5. Serve the pasta with the sauce, chopped peanuts, and cilantro.

CORN-AVOCADO
TACOS

Pears & Cream

BERRIES &
APPLE

RICE NOODLES WITH VEGGIES & PEANUT SAUCE

M E A L
P R E P

*for the rest of
the week*

Cook the Black Beans (if using dried)

You will need 2½ cups cooked black beans. If using canned beans, you'll need 2 cans, no preparation needed. If starting with dried, cook 1¼ cups beans as described on page 29. Let cool and then store in an airtight container in the refrigerator.

Cook the Brown Rice

You will need 2½ cups cooked rice. Cook 1 cup rice as described on page 29. Let cool and then store in an airtight container in the refrigerator.

Make the Boiled Potatoes and Cauliflower

Dice 4 potatoes into about 1-inch pieces. You should have 4 cups. Boil in salted water for about 25 minutes or until tender. After about 15 minutes, add 1 cup cauliflower florets; boil the cauliflower and potatoes together for the remaining 10 minutes. Drain and separate the cauliflower and potatoes. You'll need the cauliflower and 2 cups boiled potatoes for the Potato-Cauliflower Mash (right), 1 cup potatoes on their own, and another 1 cup potatoes for the Cheezy Sauce (page 56).

Make the Potato-Cauliflower Mash

Makes 2 servings

1 garlic clove, minced

1 tablespoon olive oil

2 cups Boiled Potatoes (left)

2 cups Boiled Cauliflower (left)

¼ cup cashews, soaked (see page 29)

2 tablespoon cornstarch (or ground flaxseed)

Pinch of sea salt

Pinch of ground black pepper

2 tablespoons nutritional yeast

1. Sauté the garlic in the oil in a pot over medium heat for 2 minutes.

2. Add all of the remaining ingredients and stir well. Continue to cook for another 1 to 2 minutes.

3. Mash using your blender's pulse function, an immersion blender, or a potato masher.

4. Let cool and store in an airtight container in the fridge.

Notes:

Make sure the Boiled Cauliflower is drained and patted dry with a kitchen towel.

If you happen to have nutmeg in your pantry, feel free to add a little of it to the mash.

· CONTINUES ·

COOKED VEGGIE MIX 2

Cooked Brown Rice

Curried Pumpkin
Seeds

COOKED BLACK BEANS

POTATO-CAULIFLOWER
MASH

BOILED POTATOES

CHEEZY SAUCE

Cheezy Sauce

Makes 1 serving

1 cup Boiled Potatoes (page 54)
⅓ cup cashews, soaked in water (see page 29)
⅓ stalk celery
⅓ bell pepper
½ green onion
¼ cup water
Juice of 1 lemon
1 tablespoon nutritional yeast
2 teaspoons mustard
2 teaspoons cornstarch (optional)
½ teaspoon smoked paprika
½ garlic clove
Pinch of sea salt

1. Blend all of the ingredients in a blender until smooth.

2. Store in an airtight container in the fridge.

Cooked Veggie Mix 2

Makes 2 servings

1 cup chopped cauliflower
1 cup chopped broccoli
1 tablespoon olive oil
2 cups shredded kale
Pinch of sea salt
Pinch of ground black pepper

1. Sauté the cauliflower and broccoli in the oil in a pan on medium heat for 7 minutes.

2. Add the kale, salt, and pepper and cook for 2 more minutes.

3. Let cool and store in an airtight container in the fridge.

Curried Pumpkin Seeds

Makes 3 servings

3 tablespoons pumpkin seeds
1 teaspoon curry powder
1 teaspoon olive oil
Pinch of sea salt

1. Mix all of the ingredients and toast in a small pan over high heat for 2 minutes (make sure it doesn't burn).

2. Let cool and store in an airtight container at room temperature.

Prep the Overnight Oats for Day 5

¾ cup almond milk
½ cup oats
2 teaspoons maple syrup

1. Mix the almond milk, oats, and maple syrup in a jar, then let sit overnight.

CURRIED PUMPKIN SEEDS

Day 5

"The most regretful people on earth are those who felt the call to creative work, who felt their own creative power restive and uprising, and gave to it neither power nor time."

—Mary Oliver, American poet

BREAKFAST

Overnight Oats

593 calories

Prep time: 2 minutes
Total time: 2 minutes

Overnight Oats mixture (page 56)
2 tablespoons peanut butter
1 pear, sliced
⅓ cup fresh blackberries
3 tablespoons dried cranberries

1. Combine all of the ingredients in a bowl and enjoy!

SNACK

Fruit
202 calories
1 mango

LUNCH

Potato-Veggie Bowl

577 calories

Prep time: 2 minutes
Total time: 2 minutes (add 2 to 3 minutes if you choose to reheat the potatoes and veggie mix)

Dressing
2 tablespoons mustard
1 tablespoon maple syrup

Base
1 serving Cooked Veggie Mix 2 (page 56)
1 cup Boiled Potatoes (page 54)

Toppings
1 avocado, sliced or diced
1 tablespoon Curried Pumpkin Seeds (page 56)

1. Mix the dressing ingredients together using a fork or whisk.

2. Combine the veggies and potatoes in a bowl.

3. Top with the dressing, avocado, and pumpkin seeds and enjoy!

DINNER

Green Bean Plate with Potato-Cauliflower Mash

611 calories

Prep time: 2 minutes
Cook time: 5 minutes
Total time: 7 minutes

1 cup green beans
1 garlic clove, minced
2 teaspoons olive oil
1 cup Cooked Black Beans (page 54)
Sea salt and ground black pepper, to taste
1 serving Potato-Cauliflower Mash (page 54)
1 tablespoon sunflower seeds

1. Sauté the green beans and garlic in the oil in a pan over medium heat for 5 minutes.

2. Add the black beans to the pan and cook for another 2 minutes.

3. Season with salt and pepper and serve with the mash and sunflower seeds.

Overnight Oats

POTATO-VEGGIE BOWL

MANGO

Potato-Cauliflower Mash

GREEN BEAN PLATE

Day 6

"If we think our job here on earth is to fix ourselves, we will keep looking for the broken places. If we believe our job is to be kind, we will keep lavishing love on ourselves."
—Geneen Roth, author and expert on compulsive eating

SNACK

Fruit & Peanut Butter
403 calories

2 bananas

2 tablespoons peanut butter

WEEK 1

BREAKFAST

Savory Breakfast Bowl
523 calories

Prep time: 2 minutes

Total time: 2 minutes (add 2 to 3 minutes if you choose to reheat the brown rice and black beans)

½ cup Cooked Brown Rice (page 54)

½ cup Cooked Black Beans (page 54)

1 avocado, sliced or diced

1 tablespoon Curried Pumpkin Seeds (page 56)

1. Combine all of the ingredients in a bowl and enjoy!

LUNCH

Portobello Mushroom Bowl
489 calories

Prep time: 2 minutes

Cook time: 4 minutes

Total time: 6 minutes

1 large portobello mushroom, sliced

2 tablespoons olive oil

Sea salt and ground black pepper, to taste

Pinch of smoked paprika

2 cups shredded kale

1 garlic clove, minced

1 serving Potato-Cauliflower Mash (page 54)

Fresh herbs of your choice, for garnish (optional)

1. Cook the mushrooms and 1 tablespoon of the oil, some salt and pepper, and the paprika in a pan over high heat for 3 to 4 minutes.

2. In a separate pan, cook the kale and garlic in the remaining 1 tablespoon oil over medium heat for 3 minutes.

3. Serve with the mash and garnish with the herbs.

DINNER

Stuffed Bell Peppers
598 calories

Prep time: 2 minutes

Cook time: 10 minutes

Total time: 12 minutes

2 bell peppers, hollowed out

1 cup Cooked Brown Rice (page 54)

1 serving Cooked Veggie Mix 2 (page 56)

1 serving Cheezy Sauce (page 56)

1. Preheat the oven to 425°F/ 218°C (optional; you can also eat the peppers raw). If desired, bake the bell peppers for 10 minutes.

2. Meanwhile, reheat the rice and the veggie mix together in a pot for a few minutes.

3. Fill the peppers with the rice and veggie mix and top with the sauce.

SAVORY
BREAKFAST
BOWL

PORTOBELLO MUSHROOM BOWL

*Bananas & Peanut
Butter*

STUFFED
BELL
PEPPERS

Day 7

"Some changes look negative on the surface but you will soon realize that space is being created in your life for something new to emerge."

—Eckhart Tolle, spiritual teacher and author

BREAKFAST

Jumbo Green Smoothie

495 calories

Prep time: 2 minutes
Total time: 2 minutes

3 frozen bananas
½ small (or ¼ large) zucchini
1 cup kale
½ celery stalk
1 tablespoon peanut butter
2 teaspoons ground flaxseed
1 cup almond milk

1. Blend all of the ingredients until they've reached a smooth consistency. Enjoy!

LUNCH

Black Bean Tacos

619 calories

Prep time: 2 minutes
Total time: 2 minutes (add 2 to 3 minutes if you choose to reheat the beans and rice)

3 soft corn tortillas
1 cup Cooked Black Beans (see page 54)
½ cup Cooked Brown Rice (see page 54)
2 cups chopped kale
1 tablespoon Curried Pumpkin Seeds (page 56)
Fresh herbs of your choice, for garnish (optional)

1. Fill the tortillas with all the remaining ingredients and enjoy!

DINNER

Kale-Lemon Salad

612 calories

Prep time: 2 minutes
Total time: 2 minutes

Salad
½ avocado, mashed
3 cups shredded kale
2 radishes, thinly sliced (optional)
¼ cucumber, diced
⅓ cup cherry or grape tomatoes, halved
3 tablespoons sunflower seeds
3 tablespoons dried cranberries

Dressing
Juice of 1 lemon
1 tablespoon olive oil
2 teaspoons apple cider vinegar (optional)
Pinch of sea salt

1. In a bowl, massage the avocado into the kale. Add the remaining salad ingredients.

2. Mix the dressing ingredients using a fork or whisk.

3. Combine the salad and dressing and enjoy!

SNACK

Fruit & Nuts

278 calories

2 apples
2 tablespoons cashews

Jumbo Green Smoothie

BLACK BEAN TACOS

APPLES & CASHEWS

KALE-LEMON SALAD

End of Week One:
JOURNALING EXERCISE

What was the best thing about
this week?

....

What did I learn about myself this week?

....

What did I learn about my eating habits
this week?

....

What am I proudest of this week?

....

What could I improve next week?

....

What is my number-one goal
for next week?

Week Two

SHOPPING LIST

FRUITS

Oranges	2
Apples	2
Limes	2
Blueberries	1 pint
Bananas	6
Plums	5
Grapes	1 bag (about 8 cups)
Meyer lemons (or any type of lemon)	3
Pineapple	1
Cherry tomatoes	1 pint
Tomatoes (you can also opt to get just either cherry tomatoes or regular tomatoes)	5
Avocados	4

DRIED FRUIT

Raisins	1 pack (any size)

FROZEN FRUITS

Blueberries (or any other frozen berries)	1 package
Peach slices (or frozen mango chunks)	1 package

VEGETABLES

Zucchini	3
Kabocha squash (acorn or butternut squash will work too)	1 small
Arugula	1 package
Artichoke hearts	1 jar
Lacinato or curly kale (or spinach or collard greens)	1 bunch
Radishes	1 bunch
Red onions	2
Green onions	1 bunch (about 5 green onions)
Butter lettuce	1 head
Shiitake mushrooms (or other mushrooms)	2 ounces (about ½ cup)
Carrots	6 medium
Garlic	1 head
Cucumber	1
Brussels sprouts	12 ounces (about 2 cups)
Red bell pepper	1
Chard	1 bunch
Potatoes	2 medium or 5 or 6 small (you'll need 1 cup chopped)
Sweet corn kernels	one 15-ounce can (or 1 bag frozen)

FRESH HERBS

Basil	1 bunch
Parsley	1 bunch
Chives*	1 bunch or package

LEGUMES

White beans	two 15-ounce cans or 8 ounces (1 cup) dried
Kidney beans	one 15-ounce can or 4 ounces (½ cup) dried
Chickpeas	two 15-ounce cans or 8 ounces (1 cup) dried
French lentils (green, yellow, or red lentils will work as well)	6 ounces (¾ cup) dried

NUTS & SEEDS

Hazelnuts*	2.5 ounces
Sunflower seeds	5.5 ounces
Peanut butter	1 jar
Cashews	6.5 ounces

GRAINS

Quick-cooking oats	1 container (you'll need just over 1½ cups)
Wild rice (or any kind of rice)	5 ounces
Sandwich bread or gluten-free bread	1 loaf (you'll need 6 slices)
Brown rice noodles	1 package
Quinoa*	3 ounces

CONDIMENTS & STAPLE FOODS

Cayenne pepper*	Smoked paprika*
Yellow mustard*	Sea salt
Liquid smoke*	Ground black pepper
Vegetable broth* (or vegetable bouillon paste like Better Than Bouillon)	Apple cider vinegar*
	Maple syrup
Olive oil	Crushed red pepper flakes*

MYLK

Unsweetened almond milk	1 quart

DAY 8

Breakfast Blueberry Granola Bowl

Lunch Avocado-Kale Salad

Snack Fruit

Dinner White Bean–Squash Bowl

DAY 9

Breakfast Tropical Creamsicle Smoothie Bowl

Lunch Lentil Bowl with White Bean Dip

Snack Fruit

Dinner Pineapple Fried Wild Rice

DAY 10

Breakfast Plum Granola

Lunch Herbed Lentils & Lemon-Kissed Brussels Sprouts

Snack Veggies & Seeds

Dinner Baked Potatoes with Creamy Corn Sauce

DAY 11

Breakfast Cucumber-Banana Milkshake

Lunch Crisp Cucumber & Quinoa Salad

Snack Veggies & Dip

Dinner Kidney Bean Bowl with Candied Radishes

DAY 12

Breakfast Banana-Berry-Peach Smoothie

Lunch Cashew & Avocado Sandwich

Snack Grapes

Dinner Shiitake Rice Bowl

DAY 13

Breakfast Peanut Butter Toast with Berries & Almond Milk

Lunch Brown Rice Pasta with Artichokes

Snack Veggies & Nuts

Dinner Chickpea Zucchini Boats

DAY 14

Breakfast Banana Granola

Lunch Chickpea Salad

Snack Fruit & Peanut Butter

Dinner Brown Rice Pasta with Zucchini

Week Two
MENU

Day 7 MEAL PREP

Make the Baked Potatoes & Baked Kabocha Squash

Makes 1 serving potatoes
and 2 servings squash

1 cup potatoes (if they're small, leave them whole; if they're large, cut them into chunks)
1 small kabocha squash, seeds removed, sliced

1. Preheat the oven to 400°F/ 200°C. Line one or two baking sheets with parchment paper.

2. Spread the potatoes and squash on the baking sheets and bake for 45 minutes.

3. Let cool, then store, separately, in the refrigerator in airtight containers.

Note: If you have a large kabocha squash, you can bake all of it, then store half in the freezer for future use. The skin is edible.

Make the Granola

Makes 3 servings

You can prepare this while the potatoes and squash are baking, and put it in the oven with the squash and potatoes for the last 15 minutes of their baking time.

1½ cups quick-cooking oats
¾ cup raisins
¼ cup chopped cashews
¼ cup hazelnuts
¼ cup sunflower seeds
⅓ cup maple syrup
Pinch of sea salt

1. If needed, preheat the oven to 400°F/200°C. Line a baking sheet with parchment paper.

2. Mix all of the ingredients in a bowl using a fork or spoon. Make sure the maple syrup is thoroughly mixed in.

3. Spread the granola on the baking sheet.

4. Bake for 15 minutes. Let cool, then store in an airtight container at room temperature.

Cook the White Beans (if using dried)

You will need 1½ cups cooked white beans. If using canned, you'll need 1 can, no preparation needed. If starting with dried, cook ¾ cup beans as described on page 29. Let cool and then store in an airtight container in the refrigerator.

Cook the Kidney Beans (if using dried)

You will need 1 cup cooked kidney beans. If using canned, you'll need 1 can, no preparation needed. If starting with dried, cook ½ cup beans as described on page 29. Let cool and then store in an airtight container in the refrigerator.

· CONTINUES ·

BAKED POTATOES & BAKED
KABOCHA SQUASH

COOKED WILD RICE

*Lemon-Kissed
Brussels Sprouts*

COOKED QUINOA

GRANOLA

LEMON
VINAIGRETTE

HERBED LENTILS

FROZEN BANANAS

WHITE BEAN
DIP

Cook the Brown Rice

You will need 2½ cups cooked rice. Cook 1 cup rice as described on page 29. Let cool and then store in an airtight container in the refrigerator.

Cook the Quinoa

Cook ½ cup dry quinoa as described on page 29; you will have 1½ cups. Let cool and then store in an airtight container in the refrigerator.

Cook the Wild Rice

Cook ½ cup wild rice as described on page 29; you will have 1½ cups. Let cool and then store in an airtight container in the refrigerator.

Make the Herbed Lentils

Makes 2 servings

2 tablespoons olive oil
1 large red onion, chopped
¾ cup dried French lentils
2 garlic cloves, minced
2 cups vegetable broth, or 2 cups water mixed with 2 teaspoons veggie bouillon paste
3 tablespoons liquid smoke (optional)
2 handfuls chopped parsley
2 green onions, tops only, chopped
Handful of fresh chives, chopped
½ teaspoon sea salt

1. In a large pot or pan, heat the olive oil over medium heat. Add the red onion, lentils, and garlic and cook for about 5 minutes, stirring well.

2. Add the vegetable broth. Cook over medium to high heat for another 20 minutes.

3. Add the liquid smoke, if using, and mix thoroughly.

4. Remove the pan from the stove and add the parsley, green onions, chives, and salt.

5. Let cool, then store in an airtight container in a refrigerator.

Tip: Instead of chopping the parsley with a knife, you can use scissors to cut the parsley directly into the pot.

Make the Lemon-Kissed Brussels Sprouts

Makes 2 servings

2 teaspoons olive oil
2 cups Brussels sprouts, stems removed, cut into halves
2 green onions, white parts only, chopped
½ teaspoon sea salt
Zest and juice of 1 Meyer lemon (see Note)

1. Place the oil, Brussels sprouts, green onions, and salt in a pot. Cook over medium heat for 4 minutes, stirring well.

2. Add the lemon juice. Reduce the heat to low, and cook for an additional 5 minutes.

3. Let cool, then store in an airtight container in the refrigerator.

Note: Only use the lemon zest if you're using an organic lemon. If not, use the juice only.

Make the Lemon Vinaigrette

Makes 3 servings

¼ cup apple cider vinegar
Juice of 1 Meyer lemon
¼ cup olive oil
¼ cup yellow mustard
Pinch of sea salt

1. Blend all of the ingredients until smooth. Store in an airtight container in the refrigerator.

Make the White Bean Dip

Makes 2 servings

1 cup Cooked White Beans (page 68)
¼ cup sunflower seeds
1 garlic clove, peeled
Juice of 2 limes

1. Blend all of the ingredients in a blender until smooth. Store in an airtight container in the refrigerator.

Prep the Fruits & Veggies

Freeze 3 bananas. Peel the bananas before freezing them, and store in a reusable container or ziplock bag (reusable containers are more eco-friendly). Try not to cut the bananas before freezing them so they don't stick together. You'll find them very easy to cut while frozen.

Note: IMPORTANT—Bananas should be frozen when they are very ripe, that is to say, "spotty." So if your bananas aren't ripe enough on Sunday night, wait until Wednesday night to freeze them.

Feel free to cut the veggies for the snacks in advance. It's always best to cut them the day of, but if you know you won't have enough time, prepare them and store them in an airtight container in the refrigerator.

WEEK
2

Day 8

*"Being messy is not hereditary
nor is it related to lack of time."*

—Marie Kondo, author of
The Life-Changing Magic of Tidying Up

BREAKFAST

Blueberry Granola Bowl

509 calories

Prep time: 2 minutes

Total time: 2 minutes

1 serving Granola (page 68)
½ cup fresh blueberries
½ cup almond milk

1. Mix all of the ingredients together and enjoy!

SNACK

Fruit

226 calories

½ pineapple, cut into slices or chunks

LUNCH

Avocado-Kale Salad

610 calories

Prep time: 3 minutes

Total time: 3 minutes

1 avocado, diced
1 cup lacinato or curly kale
1 cup arugula
1 green onion, chopped
2 tablespoons sunflower seeds
2 tablespoons raisins
⅓ cup (1 serving) Lemon Vinaigrette (page 71)

1. In a bowl, massage the avocado into the kale and arugula.

2. Mix with all the remaining ingredients and enjoy!

Note: If you prepare this dish at the beginning of the day to eat later, be sure to keep the dressing in a separate container until you are ready to eat.

DINNER

White Bean–Squash Bowl

676 calories

Prep time: 5 minutes

Cook time: 3 minutes

Total time: 8 minutes

½ cup Cooked White Beans (page 68)
½ cup Cooked Quinoa (page 70)
1 serving Lemon-Kissed Brussels Sprouts (page 70)
1 serving Baked Kabocha Squash (page 68)
⅓ cup (1 serving) Lemon Vinaigrette (page 71)

1. Combine the beans, quinoa, Brussels sprouts, and squash in a pot or pan and reheat over medium heat for 3 minutes.

2. Transfer to a bowl and add the vinaigrette. Enjoy!

BLUEBERRY GRANOLA BOWL

Pineapple

AVOCADO-KALE
SALAD

WHITE BEAN-SQUASH BOWL

Day 9

"Act the way you want to be and soon you will be the way you act."

—Iyanla Vanzant, life coach and inspirational speaker

Fruit

149 calories

1 apple

2 tablespoons raisins

BREAKFAST

Tropical Creamsicle Smoothie Bowl

547 calories

Prep time: 2 minutes

Total time: 2 minutes

Smoothie
2½ cups frozen peach slices
2 oranges, skin and seeds removed
¼ pineapple, skin removed, chopped
½ cup almond milk

Toppings
1 tablespoon chopped hazelnuts
1 tablespoon chopped cashews
1 tablespoon raisins
1 tablespoon quick-cooking oats

1. Blend the smoothie ingredients until they reach a smooth consistency.

2. Transfer to a bowl, then add the toppings. Enjoy!

LUNCH

Lentil Bowl with White Bean Dip

649 calories

Prep time: 2 minutes

Cook time: 2 to 3 minutes

Total time: 4 to 5 minutes

1 serving Herbed Lentils (page 70)
1 serving White Bean Dip (page 71)

1. Combine the herbed lentils and white bean dip in a pan. Reheat over medium heat for 2 to 3 minutes.

2. Transfer to a bowl and enjoy!

DINNER

Pineapple Fried Wild Rice

632 calories

Prep time: 2 minutes

Cook time: 5 to 6 minutes

Total time: 7 to 8 minutes

1 tablespoon olive oil
¼ pineapple, peeled and diced
1 cup Cooked Wild Rice (page 70)
1 cup chopped kale
Pinch of sea salt
Pinch of ground black pepper
1 avocado, sliced or diced

1. Heat the oil in a pan over high heat. Add the pineapple and cook for 3 minutes, stirring well.

2. Add the wild rice and kale. Reduce the heat to medium and cook for an additional 2 to 3 minutes. Season with salt and pepper.

3. Serve with the avocado.

WEEK 2

TROPICAL CREAMSICLE SMOOTHIE BOWL

Apple &
Raisins

PINEAPPLE FRIED WILD RICE

LENTIL BOWL WITH
WHITE BEAN DIP

Day 10

*"Your life is an occasion.
Rise to it."*

—Suzanne Weyn, author

BREAKFAST

Plum Granola

593 calories

Prep time: 2 minutes
Total time: 2 minutes

1 serving Granola (page 68)
½ cup almond milk
5 plums, sliced

1. Combine the granola, almond milk, and plums in a bowl. Enjoy!

SNACK

Veggies & Seeds

294 calories

½ cucumber, sliced
⅓ cup sunflower seeds

LUNCH

Herbed Lentils & Lemon-Kissed Brussels Sprouts

560 calories

Prep time: 2 minutes
Total time: 2 minutes (add 2 to 3 minutes if you choose to reheat the lentils and Brussels sprouts)

1 serving Herbed Lentils (page 70)
1 serving Lemon-Kissed Brussels Sprouts (page 70)
2 tablespoons mustard
1 tablespoon maple syrup
Fresh parsley (or any other herb), for garnish (optional)

1. Combine the lentils and Brussels sprouts in a bowl.

2. Combine the mustard and maple syrup, drizzle over the lentil mixture, and garnish with the parsley, if using. Enjoy!

DINNER

Baked Potatoes with Creamy Corn Sauce

537 calories

Prep time: 5 minutes
Cook time: 2 minutes
Total time: 7 minutes

Baked Potatoes
1 cup Baked Potatoes (page 68)
1 cup chopped kale
1 cup arugula

Creamy Corn Sauce
1 cup corn kernels (canned or frozen; see note)
⅓ cup cashews, soaked in water (see page 29)
¼ cup water
1 garlic clove
½ teaspoon sea salt
Dash of ground black pepper

Garnish
Fresh herbs of your choice (optional)
Olive oil

1. Reheat the potatoes in a small pan over high heat for 1 to 2 minutes. (If you'd like to warm the kale, you can do that at the same time.) Put the potatoes, kale, and arugula in a bowl.

2. Blend all of the sauce ingredients until smooth. Transfer to a pot and cook over high heat for 1 to 2 minutes.

3. Pour the sauce over the veggies. Sprinkle with herbs, if using, drizzle olive oil on top, and enjoy!

Note: If using frozen corn, cook over medium heat for 1 to 2 minutes before blending.

Plum
Granola

HERBED LENTILS & LEMON-KISSED
BRUSSELS SPROUTS

CUCUMBER &
SUNFLOWER SEEDS

BAKED POTATOES WITH CREAMY CORN SAUCE

Day 11

"The greatest gift you can ever give another person is your own happiness."
—Esther Hicks, inspirational speaker and author

BREAKFAST

Cucumber-Banana Milkshake

548 calories

Prep time: 2 minutes
Total time: 2 minutes

3 frozen bananas
¼ cucumber
2 tablespoons peanut butter
¾ cup almond milk

1. Blend all of the ingredients until they reach a smooth consistency. Enjoy!

Note: This will not taste the same with non-frozen bananas, so make sure to use frozen bananas. To make blending easier, cut the frozen bananas into chunks.

LUNCH

Crisp Cucumber & Quinoa Salad

525 calories

Prep time: 2 minutes
Total time: 2 minutes

1 cup Cooked Quinoa (page 70)
1 cup arugula
3 radishes, sliced
¼ cucumber, diced
2 tablespoons sunflower seeds
⅓ cup (1 serving) Lemon Vinaigrette (page 71)
Sea salt and ground black pepper to taste

1. Mix all of the ingredients well and enjoy!

SNACK

Veggies & Dip

375 calories

2 carrots
1 red bell pepper
1 serving White Bean Dip (page 71)

DINNER

Kidney Bean Bowl with Candied Radishes

491 calories

Prep time: 3 minutes
Cook time: 5 to 6 minutes
Total time: 8 to 9 minutes

1 tablespoon olive oil
4 medium or 6 small radishes, diced
1 tablespoon maple syrup
½ teaspoon sea salt
1 cup Cooked Kidney Beans (page 68)
1 serving Baked Kabocha Squash (page 68)
1 cup arugula

1. In a pan, heat the olive oil and the radishes over high heat for 2 minutes.

2. Add the maple syrup and salt, then caramelize the radishes for 1 to 2 minutes. Reduce the heat to medium and cook for another 2 minutes.

3. In another pot or pan, reheat the kidney beans and squash for 2 minutes.

4. Serve everything over a bed of arugula.

Cucumber-Banana
Milkshake

VEGGIES & WHITE
BEAN DIP

KIDNEY BEAN BOWL WITH CANDIED RADISHES

CRISP CUCUMBER &
QUINOA SALAD

M E A L
P R E P

for the rest of the week

Cook the Chickpeas (if using dried)

You will need 2½ to 3 cups cooked chickpeas. If using canned, you'll need 2 cans, no preparation needed. If starting with dried, cook 1 cup chickpeas as described on page 29. Let cool and then store in an airtight container in the refrigerator.

Make the Spicy Cashew Dressing

Makes 3 servings

½ cup cashews, soaked in water (see page 29)
¼ cup apple cider vinegar
Juice of 1 lemon
½ clove garlic
1 teaspoon smoked paprika
¼ teaspoon chili flakes
Pinch of sea salt
Pinch of cayenne pepper (optional)

1. Blend all of the ingredients until smooth. Store in an airtight container in the refrigerator.

Make the Smoky Carrots

Makes 2 servings

4 small or 3 medium carrots
1 tablespoon liquid smoke
1 teaspoon olive oil
½ teaspoon sea salt
½ teaspoon smoked paprika

1. Preheat the oven to 400°F/ 200°C. Line a baking sheet with parchment paper.

2. Peel the carrots, cut off the ends, and slice the carrots very thinly using a sharp knife or vegetable peeler.

3. Mix the liquid smoke, olive oil, salt, and paprika in a small bowl. Mix in the carrots, making sure that the carrots are fully coated with the seasoning mixture.

4. Spread the carrots on the baking sheet. Bake for 12 to 13 minutes.

5. Let cool, then store in an airtight container at room temperature.

COOKED CHICKPEAS

SPICY CASHEW
DRESSING

Smoky
Carrots

Day 12

"Be thankful for what you have; you'll end up having more. If you concentrate on what you don't have, you will never, ever have enough."
—Oprah Winfrey

SNACK

Grapes
248 calories

4 cups grapes

BREAKFAST

Banana-Berry-Peach Smoothie

599 calories

Prep time: 3 minutes
Total time: 3 minutes

2 bananas
1 cup frozen peach slices
1 cup water
1 cup frozen blueberries
2 tablespoons peanut butter

1. Blend the bananas, peaches, water, blueberries, and peanut butter until they reach a smooth consistency.

LUNCH

Cashew & Avocado Sandwich

598 calories

Prep time: 3 minutes
Total time: 3 minutes

½ avocado
3 slices regular or gluten-free sandwich bread, toasted
½ teaspoon smoked paprika
Pinch of sea salt
½ serving Spicy Cashew Dressing (page 80)
1 cup or 2 leaves butter lettuce
1 tomato, sliced
1 serving Smoky Carrots (page 80)

1. Mash the avocado and spread on one slice of toast. Sprinkle with the smoked paprika and salt. Top with a second slice of toast.

2. Spread the spicy cashew dressing on top of the second slice of toast. Add the lettuce, tomato, and carrots. Top with the remaining slice of toast and enjoy!

DINNER

Shiitake Rice Bowl

562 calories

Prep time: 2 minutes
Cook time: 4 minutes
Total time: 6 minutes

1 tablespoon olive oil
½ cup sliced shiitake mushrooms
½ cup Cooked Wild Rice (page 70)
½ cup Cooked Chickpeas (page 80)
1½ cups chopped chard
Sea salt and ground black pepper, to taste
1½ servings Spicy Cashew Dressing (page 80)

1. Heat the oil and mushrooms in a pan over high heat for 1 minute.

2. Reduce the heat to medium, then add the rice, chickpeas, and chard. Season with salt and pepper. Cook for 3 minutes.

3. Stir well, then transfer to a bowl and serve with the dressing.

WEEK 2

BANANA-BERRY-
PEACH SMOOTHIE

GRAPES

SHIITAKE RICE BOWL

Cashew & Avocado
Sandwich

Day 13

*"Out beyond ideas of wrongdoing
and rightdoing there is a field.
I'll meet you there."*

—Rumi, Persian poet

BREAKFAST

Peanut Butter Toast with Berries & Almond Milk

587 calories

Prep time: 2 minutes

Total time: 2 minutes

3 tablespoons peanut butter

2 slices regular or gluten-free bread, toasted

½ cup fresh blueberries

1 cup almond milk

1. Spread the peanut butter on the toast and top with the blueberries. Enjoy with the almond milk on the side.

SNACK

Grapes

248 calories

4 cups grapes

LUNCH

Brown Rice Pasta with Artichokes

517 calories

Prep time: 2 minutes

Cook time: 8 to 11 minutes

Total time: 10 to 13 minutes

2 ounces dried brown rice pasta (about ½ cup)

1 tablespoon olive oil

5 or 6 artichoke hearts (from 1 can or jar), drained

½ cup diced tomatoes

Handful of fresh basil leaves

2 tablespoons sunflower seeds

Sea salt and ground black pepper, to taste

1. Cook the pasta according to the package instructions (this usually takes 3 to 6 minutes depending on which brand you use).

2. Meanwhile, in a separate pan, heat the oil over medium heat. Add the artichokes and cook for 5 minutes.

3. Combine the pasta and artichokes. Stir in the tomatoes, basil, and sunflower seeds, season with salt and pepper, then enjoy!

DINNER

Chickpea Zucchini Boats

603 calories

Prep time: 3 minutes

Cook time: 4 minutes

Total time: 7 minutes

2 zucchini

1 teaspoon olive oil

1 cup chopped chard

1 cup Cooked Chickpeas (page 80)

¼ cup cherry tomatoes, sliced or chopped

2 teaspoons sunflower seeds, to garnish

Fresh herbs of your choice, for garnish

1 serving Spicy Cashew Dressing (page 80)

1. Cut each zucchini in half lengthwise. Using a small spoon, carve out the inside of the zucchini.

2. In a large pan, heat the oil over medium to high heat. Cook the zucchini shells for 2 minutes, then flip and cook for an additional 2 minutes.

3. Meanwhile, in a small pot, cook the chard and chickpeas over medium heat for 3 minutes.

4. Fill the zucchini boats with the chard-chickpea mixture. Top with the cherry tomatoes and sunflower seeds. Garnish with the herbs. Serve with the cashew dressing.

Note: You can save the carved-out zucchini to use in a smoothie later.

PEANUT BUTTER
TOAST WITH BERRIES
& ALMOND MILK

GRAPES

BROWN RICE PASTA WITH ARTICHOKES

Chickpea Zucchini
Boats

Day 14

"I am no longer accepting the things I cannot change. I am changing the things I cannot accept."

—Angela Davis, activist and author

BREAKFAST

Banana Granola

572 calories

Prep time: 2 minutes
Total time: 2 minutes

1 serving Granola (page 68)
1 banana, sliced
½ cup almond milk

1. Combine the granola, banana, and almond milk in a bowl. Enjoy!

SNACK

Fruit & Peanut Butter

191 calories

1 apple
1 tablespoon peanut butter

LUNCH

Chickpea Salad

665 calories

Prep time: 3 minutes
Total time: 3 minutes (add 2 to 3 minutes if you choose to heat up the chickpeas)

1 avocado
2 cups butter lettuce, torn
1 cup Cooked Chickpeas (page 80)
2 medium-sized tomatoes, chopped or sliced
1 slice regular or gluten-free bread, toasted and cut into crouton-sized bites
Fresh herbs of your choice, for garnish (optional)

1. Mash the avocado in a large bowl. Mix in the lettuce, chickpeas, tomatoes, and croutons.

2. Garnish with the herbs, if using, and enjoy!

DINNER

Brown Rice Pasta with Zucchini

556 calories

Prep time: 3 minutes
Cook time: 10 to 13 minutes
Total time: 13 to 16 minutes

2 ounces dried brown rice pasta (about ½ cup)
1 red onion, sliced
1 zucchini, sliced
1 garlic clove, thinly sliced
2 teaspoons olive oil
1 tablespoon cashews
1 tablespoon maple syrup
Sea salt and ground black pepper, to taste
1 serving Smoky Carrots (page 80)

1. Cook the pasta according to the package instructions (this usually takes 3 to 6 minutes depending on which brand you use).

2. While the pasta is cooking, in a separate pan, cook the onion, zucchini, and garlic in the oil over medium heat for 5 minutes. Add the cashews and maple syrup, season with salt and pepper, and cook for an additional 2 minutes.

3. Combine the pasta and veggie mixture, then top with the smoky carrots.

Note: The onions will be a bit crisp. If you'd like them to have a softer texture, cook them with the olive oil for 5 minutes before adding the zucchini and garlic.

Banana Granola

CHICKPEA SALAD

APPLE & PEANUT
BUTTER

BROWN RICE PASTA
WITH ZUCCHINI

End of Week Two:

JOURNALING EXERCISE

What was the best thing about this week?

....

What did I learn about myself this week?

....

What did I learn about my eating habits
this week?

....

What am I proudest of this week?

....

What could I improve next week?

....

What is my number-one goal for next week?

....

Week Three
SHOPPING LIST

Note: You may already have some of the items listed, so make sure you check your pantry before shopping.

FRUITS

Kiwis	3
Apples	3
Bananas	9
Fresh blueberries, or frozen	1 pint
Small tomatoes	7
Cherry tomatoes*	1 pint
Avocados	3
Limes	5
Frozen blueberries	1 bag
Frozen mango	1 bag

DRIED FRUIT

Unsweetened coconut flakes (not shredded)	1 bag

VEGETABLES

Large white onions	2
Red onion	1
Garlic	1 bulb
Zucchini	1
Small cauliflower head	1
Bell peppers	4 or 5
Celery	1 bunch
Green onions	1 bunch

Mixed mushrooms	1 cup, sliced
Sweet potato	2 small or 1 large
Potatoes	3 medium
Carrots	1 small bag or bunch
Butternut squash	1
Baby bok choy	1 head
Corn kernels	one 14-ounce can (or use frozen)

FRESH GREENS

Part 1:

Mixed greens	1 bag
Collard greens	1 bunch

Part 2 *(if you can, get these on Thursday to ensure they're as fresh as possible):*

Arugula	1 bag
Swiss chard	1 bunch

FRESH HERBS & ROOTS

Cilantro	1 bunch
Lemongrass*	1 bunch
Fresh ginger*	1 piece

LEGUMES

Yellow lentils	8 ounces (1 cup) dried
Black beans	three 15-ounce cans or 1 pound (2 cups) dried
Extra-firm tofu	1 pack (15 ounces)
Chickpeas	two or three 15-ounce cans or 1 pound (2 cups) dried

NUTS & SEEDS

Walnuts	4 ounces
Sliced almonds	3 ounces

Cashews	6 ounces
Tahini	1 jar
Peanut butter	1 jar

GRAINS

Sushi rice (or short-grain rice)	12 ounces (1⅓ cups) dry
Store-bought or homemade vegan granola	½ cup
Quick-cooking oats	3 ounces (¾ cup) dry
Corn tortillas	1 pack

CONDIMENTS & STAPLE FOODS

Olive oil	Yellow or Dijon mustard
Vegetable broth or veggie bouillon paste	Nutritional yeast
Tamari or soy sauce	Rice paper* (1 pack; optional)
Maple syrup	Tomato paste
	Cacao powder*

SPICES

Smoked paprika (or regular paprika)	Ground cinnamon*
Liquid smoke (or smoked salt)*	Sea salt
Ground turmeric* (or curry powder or saffron)	Ground black pepper

MYLK

Unsweetened cashew milk (or any other plant-based milk)	1 quart
Full-fat coconut milk (for cooking)	one 14-ounce can
Unsweetened coconut yogurt	8 ounces (1 cup)

DAY 15

Breakfast Turmeric-Tofu Scramble
on Corn Tortilla

Lunch Burrito Bowl

Snack Fruit & Nut Butter

Dinner Black Bean Tortillas

DAY 16

Breakfast Overnight Oats

Lunch Tortilla Bean Salad

Snack Veggies & Tahini

Dinner Tofu & Rice Spring Rolls
with Peanut Dip

DAY 17

Breakfast Blueberry-Banana
Ice Cream

Lunch Spring Roll Bowl

Snack Fruit & Nuts

Dinner Creamy Corn-Tomato Soup

DAY 18

Breakfast Apple-Cinnamon
Rice Pudding

Lunch Chickpea & Root
Veggie Bowl

Snack Fruit & Nut Butter

Dinner Bok Choy Miso Soup

DAY 19

Breakfast Coco Mango Froyo

Lunch Chickpea & Arugula Salad

Snack Veggies & Seed Butter

Dinner Mushroom Rice Bowl

DAY 20

Breakfast Chocolate Granola

Lunch Potato Bake on
a Bed of Arugula

Snack Fruit & Nuts

Dinner Coconut Lentil Soup

DAY 21

Breakfast Banana-Chocolate Shake

Lunch Yellow Lentil Bowl

Snack Veggies & Seed Butter

Dinner Potato Bake & Swiss Chard

Week Three

MENU

Make the Coconut Bacon & Maple Pumpkin Seeds

Makes 3 servings (2 tablespoons each) of coconut bacon and 1½ servings (2 tablespoons each) of maple pumpkin seeds

Liquid Mix Ingredients
2 teaspoons liquid smoke
2 teaspoons maple syrup
2 teaspoons tamari or soy sauce
½ teaspoon smoked paprika
Dash of sea salt

Dry ingredients
6 tablespoons unsweetened coconut flakes
6 tablespoons pumpkin seeds

1. Preheat the oven to 300°F/ 150°C. Line a baking sheet with parchment paper (or use two baking sheets).

2. Combine all of the liquid mix ingredients. Put the coconut flakes and the pumpkin seeds in separate bowls. Mix half of the liquid mix with the coconut flakes and the other half with the pumpkin seeds.

3. Spread the coconut flakes and the pumpkin seeds evenly across the baking sheet, keeping them separated (or spread them on two baking sheets). Bake for 10 minutes.

4. Let cool and then store separately in airtight containers at room temperature.

Cook the Black Beans (if using dried)

You'll need 2 cups cooked black beans. If using canned, you'll need 2 cans, no preparation needed. If starting with dried, cook ⅔ cup beans as described on page 29. Let cool and then store in an airtight container in the refrigerator.

Cook the Rice

I recommend sushi rice, because it's the kind of rice that works best in rice pudding, but feel free to use any other kind of rice. You will need 4 cups cooked rice. Cook 1½ cups rice as described on page 29. Let cool and then store in an airtight container in the refrigerator.

Make the Baked Root Veggie Mix

This recipe makes 4 servings (1 cup each), and the root veggies will keep for 7 to 8 days in the fridge. You'll need 2 servings for Days 16 and 18 and another 2 servings for Days 20 and 21. Since you'll be baking another dish on Day 18 anyway, you can split this in half and bake 2 servings on Day 14 and 2 servings on Day 18. Either way works depending on what will be most convenient for you.

2 cups diced butternut squash
2 cups diced sweet potatoes

1. Preheat the oven to 400°F/ 200°C. Line a baking sheet with parchment paper.

2. Spread the root veggies on the baking sheet. Bake for 45 minutes.

3. Let cool and then store in an airtight container in the fridge.

Note: You can peel the veggies, but you don't need to.

· CONTINUES ·

COOKED BLACK BEANS

COCONUT BACON

TURMERIC-TOFU SCRAMBLE

COOKED VEGGIE MIX

SMOKY KETCHUP

Cooked Rice

SALSA

BAKED ROOT VEGGIE MIX

MAPLE PUMPKIN SEEDS

Tofu Mix

Frozen Bananas

Make the Cooked Veggie Mix

Makes 4 servings

2 tablespoons olive oil
2 large onions, chopped
2 garlic cloves, minced
2 celery stalks, chopped
1 large carrot, chopped
2½ cups chopped cauliflower
1 bell pepper, sliced or chopped
¼ cup vegetable broth, or ¼ cup water mixed with ¼ teaspoon veggie bouillon paste

1. Heat the olive oil in a large pot over medium heat. Add the onions and garlic and cook for 5 minutes.

2. Add the celery, carrot, cauliflower, bell pepper, and broth and mix well. Turn the heat down to medium-low and cook for another 15 minutes.

3. Strain the veggie mixture to remove excess liquid. Let cool and then store in an airtight container in the fridge.

Cook the Tofu Mix

Makes 2 servings

1 tablespoon olive oil
2 green onions, chopped
1 garlic clove, minced
10 ounces extra-firm tofu, diced
½ inch lemongrass, very thinly sliced (see Note; optional)
2 tablespoons sliced almonds
1 teaspoon grated fresh ginger
Sea salt and ground black pepper to taste

1. Heat the olive oil in a pan over high heat. Add the green onions and garlic and cook for 2 minutes.

2. Reduce the heat to medium and add the tofu, lemongrass (if using), almonds, and ginger; season with salt and pepper. Cook for another 6 to 7 minutes.

3. Let cool and then store in an airtight container in the fridge.

Note: To slice lemongrass, cut off the thick end and remove 2 or 3 of the thin outer layers. Then slice the lemongrass very thinly using a sharp knife.

Cook the Turmeric-Tofu Scramble

Makes 1 serving

1 teaspoon olive oil
5 ounces extra-firm tofu, diced
½ bell pepper, sliced or chopped
1 green onion, chopped
1 garlic clove, minced
½ teaspoon ground turmeric

1. Combine all of the ingredients in a large pan and cook for 7 minutes over medium heat. Use a fork to "scramble" the tofu while cooking. Stir well.

2. Let cool and store in an airtight container in the fridge.

Notes:
1. Depending on your schedule, you can skip this and simply make the scramble in the morning on Day 15.

2. The turmeric is included to make the scramble yellow. You can use curry powder or saffron instead, although curry will change the taste, while turmeric and saffron are a little more neutral in flavor.

3. Tofu is sold in a package containing a lot of liquid. Remove some of the excess liquid by gently pressing the tofu block with a kitchen towel.

Make the Salsa

Makes 4 servings

3 tomatoes, diced
1 green onion, chopped
⅓ red onion, very finely chopped
¼ cup fresh cilantro, chopped
Juice of 1 lime

1. Mix all of the ingredients well and store in a jar in the fridge.

Make the Smoky Ketchup

Makes 3 servings

1 teaspoon olive oil
1 green onion, chopped
½ garlic clove, minced
1 small can (6 ounces) tomato paste
2 to 3 tablespoons water
2 tablespoons liquid smoke
2 tablespoons maple syrup
1 tablespoon tamari or soy sauce
2 teaspoons mustard
½ teaspoon smoked paprika
Dash of sea salt

1. Heat the olive oil, green onion, and garlic in a small pot over high heat and cook for 2 minutes.

2. Reduce the heat to medium and add all of the remaining ingredients. Mix well, until the consistency is smooth, and cook for another 4 to 5 minutes.

3. Let cool and store in a jar in the fridge.

Prep the Fruits & Veggies

1. Freeze 5 bananas: Peel the bananas before freezing them, and store in a reusable container or ziplock bag (reusable containers are more eco-friendly). Try not to cut the bananas before freezing them so they don't stick together. You'll find them very easy to cut while frozen.

2. Cut the veggies (optional): In order to save time during the week, you can prep the veggies you'll need for the spring rolls and snacks.

WEEK
3

Day 15

1,970 CALORIES

"The other important thing to understand is that as humans we see only a segment of reality in the greater cosmic scheme of things, so we are really never in a position to judge anyone or anything."

—Karen Kingston, feng shui expert

SNACK

Fruit & Nut Butter

306 calories

2 bananas
1 tablespoon peanut butter

BREAKFAST

Turmeric-Tofu Scramble on Corn Tortilla

497 calories

Prep time: 2 minutes
Cook time: 2 to 5 minutes
Total time: 4 to 7 minutes

1 corn tortilla
1 serving Turmeric-Tofu Scramble (page 94)
½ avocado, sliced or diced
½ handful of fresh cilantro leaves
1 serving Salsa (page 95)
1 serving Smoky Ketchup (page 95)

1. Heat the tortilla in the oven, in a skillet, in the toaster, or in the microwave.

2. Reheat the tofu scramble at the same time.

3. Fill the tortilla with the tofu scramble and serve with the avocado, cilantro, salsa, and smoky ketchup.

LUNCH

Burrito Bowl

654 calories

Prep time: 2 minutes
Total time: 2 minutes (add 2 to 5 minutes if you choose to reheat the rice, beans, and veggies)

2 cups mixed greens
1 cup Cooked Sushi Rice (page 92)
½ cup Cooked Black Beans (page 92)
1 serving Cooked Veggie Mix (page 94)
⅓ avocado, sliced or diced
½ handful of fresh cilantro leaves
1 serving Salsa (page 95)
Juice of ½ lime

1. Combine all of the ingredients in a bowl and enjoy!

DINNER

Black Bean Tortillas

513 calories

Prep time: 2 minutes
Cook time: 2 to 5 minutes
Total time: 4 to 7 minutes

2 corn tortillas
1 serving Cooked Veggie Mix (page 94)
½ cup Cooked Black Beans (page 92)
1½ cups shredded collard greens
1 serving Smoky Ketchup (page 95)
1 serving Maple Pumpkin Seeds (page 92)

1. Heat the tortillas in the oven, in a skillet, in the toaster, or in the microwave.

2. Reheat the veggies and beans at the same time.

3. Fill the tortillas with the veggies, beans, and collards, and top with the ketchup and pumpkin seeds.

TURMERIC-TOFU SCRAMBLE
ON CORN TORTILLA

*Bananas
& Peanut
Butter*

BURRITO BOWL

BLACK BEAN
TORTILLAS

Day 16

"We are very afraid of being powerless. But we have the power to look deeply at our fears, and then fear cannot control us."
-Thich Nhat Hanh

BREAKFAST

Overnight Oats

462 calories

Prep time: 2 minutes
Cook time: 0 to 3 minutes
Total time: 2 to 5 minutes

You can either prepare this the night before, in which case you don't need to cook it, or the same day, in which case you simply need to cook it for 2 to 3 minutes. If you're using frozen blueberries instead of fresh, you should cook the oatmeal.

¾ cup quick-cooking oats
¾ cup cashew milk
½ cup fresh blueberries
1 tablespoon walnuts
1 tablespoon peanut butter
2 teaspoons maple syrup
Dash of sea salt

1. The night before, mix all of the ingredients in a jar and store in the fridge until morning.

LUNCH

Tortilla Bean Salad

573 calories

Prep time: 2 minutes
Cook time: 0 to 3 minutes
Total time: 2 to 5 minutes (add 2 to 3 minutes if you choose to reheat the beans)

1 corn tortilla
1 serving Baked Root Veggie Mix (page 92)
1 cup Cooked Black Beans (page 92)
1 cup mixed greens
1 cup shredded collard greens
1 serving Coconut Bacon (page 92)
1 serving Salsa (page 95)

1. Heat the tortilla in the oven, in a skillet, in the toaster, or in the microwave.

2. Fill it with the root veggies, beans, mixed greens, and collards and top with the coconut bacon and salsa.

DINNER

Tofu & Rice Spring Rolls with Peanut Dip

732 calories

Prep time: 10 to 15 minutes
Total time: 10 to 15 minutes (if you choose to omit the rice paper rolls, the prep time is 3 to 5 minutes total)

Spring Rolls
10 rice paper wrappers
2 cups mixed greens
2 carrots, grated or thinly sliced
1 bell pepper, thinly sliced
1 serving Tofu Mix (page 94)
1 cup Cooked Sushi Rice (page 92)

Peanut Dip
4 tablespoons peanut butter
Juice of 2 limes
Dash of sea salt
2 tablespoons tamari or soy sauce
2 tablespoons water

1. Wet each rice paper wrapper with water and let soften for 1 to 2 minutes. Place each wrapper on a plate, and arrange the greens, carrots, bell pepper, tofu, and rice down the middle. Fold over the ends and then wrap them into spring rolls.

2. Mix all of the dip ingredients using a fork or a whisk.

3. Set half of the spring rolls and half of the peanut dip aside for tomorrow's lunch. Enjoy the remaining spring rolls and dip.

Note: The leftover peanut dip will separate. Mix it well once more the next day before serving.

Overnight Oats

TORTILLA BEAN SALAD

Celery & Tahini

TOFU & RICE SPRING ROLLS
WITH PEANUT DIP

Veggies & Tahini

202 calories

4 celery stalks
2 tablespoons tahini

Note: Feel free to mix some
lime or lemon juice and water
into the tahini if you don't like
the taste by itself.

SNACK

Day 17

"The animals of the world exist for their own reasons. They were not made for humans any more than black people were made for white, or women created for men."
—Alice Walker, *author*

BREAKFAST

Blueberry-Banana Ice Cream

415 calories

Prep time: 3 to 5 minutes
Total time: 3 to 5 minutes

2 frozen bananas
1 cup frozen blueberries
¼ cup cashew milk
2 tablespoons walnuts

1. Blend the bananas, blueberries, and cashew milk in a blender or food processor. You may need to cut the bananas into smaller chunks. Add more cashew milk or water if necessary.

2. Top with the walnuts and enjoy!

LUNCH

Spring Roll Bowl

746 calories

Prep time: 2 minutes
Total time: 2 minutes

1 cup mixed greens
Leftover Spring Rolls (from Day 16, page 98)
Leftover Peanut Dip (from Day 16, page 98)
1 serving Maple Pumpkin Seeds (page 92)

1. Combine the greens, spring rolls, peanut dip, and pumpkin seeds in a bowl. Enjoy!

SNACK

Fruit & Nuts

218 calories

1 apple
3 tablespoons walnuts

DINNER

Creamy Corn-Tomato Soup

614 calories

Prep time: 2 minutes
Cook time: 5 minutes
Total time: 7 minutes

4 small tomatoes, chopped
1 serving Cooked Veggie Mix (page 94)
½ cup corn (frozen or canned)
1 serving Smoky Ketchup (page 95)
1 teaspoon veggie bouillon paste
½ cup canned full-fat coconut milk (see Note)
Sea salt and ground black pepper, to taste
½ handful of fresh cilantro leaves
1 serving Coconut Bacon (page 92)

1. Place the tomatoes, veggie mix, corn, ketchup, veggie paste, and coconut milk in a small pot, mix well, and cook for 5 minutes on medium to high heat. Season with salt and pepper.

2. Transfer to a bowl and top with the cilantro and coconut bacon.

Note: Be sure to use canned coconut milk for cooking, not the carton coconut milk sold for drinking.

BLUEBERRY-
BANANA ICE
CREAM

SPRING ROLL BOWL

*Apple &
Walnuts*

CREAMY CORN-
TOMATO SOUP

Day 18

"A thought is harmless unless we believe it. It's not our thoughts, but our attachment to our thoughts, that causes suffering. Attaching to a thought means believing that it's true, without inquiring. A belief is a thought that we've been attaching to, often for years."

—Byron Katie, self-help speaker and author

BREAKFAST

Apple-Cinnamon Rice Pudding

577 calories

Prep time: 2 minutes
Cook time: 3 to 5 minutes
Total time: 5 to 7 minutes

1 cup Cooked Sushi Rice (page 92)
½ cup cashew milk
3 tablespoons cashews
1 tablespoon maple syrup
1 teaspoon ground cinnamon
1 apple

1. Cook the rice and cashew milk in a small pot over medium to high heat, stirring well, for 3 to 5 minutes. Add a little water or more cashew milk if necessary.

2. Transfer to a bowl and mix in the cashews, maple syrup, and cinnamon.

3. You can either enjoy the apple on the side or dice it and mix it into the rice pudding.

LUNCH

Chickpea & Root Veggie Bowl

576 calories

Prep time: 2 minutes
Total time: 2 minutes (add 2 to 3 minutes if you decide to reheat the chickpeas and veggies)

1 cup mixed greens
1 cup Cooked Chickpeas (page 29)
1 serving Cooked Veggie Mix (page 94)
1 serving Baked Root Veggie Mix (page 92)
1 serving Maple Pumpkin Seeds (page 92)
2 tablespoons mustard

1. Combine all of the ingredients together in a bowl and enjoy!

DINNER

Bok Choy Miso Soup

498 calories

Prep time: 2 minutes
Cook time: 9 to 10 minutes
Total time: 11 to 12 minutes

1½ cups vegetable broth, or 1½ cups water mixed with 1½ teaspoons veggie bouillon paste
1 tablespoon olive oil
2 green onions, chopped
1 head baby bok choy, either cut in half or chopped
1 serving Tofu Mix (page 94)
½ bell pepper, chopped
1 cup shredded collard greens
1 tablespoon miso paste
Handful of fresh cilantro leaves

1. Bring the broth to a boil (which will take 2 to 3 minutes).

2. In the meantime, heat the olive oil in a pot over medium heat and add the green onions.

3. Add the boiling broth, the bok choy, tofu mix, bell pepper, and collard greens. Cook for 7 minutes. Stir well, and then add the miso paste at the end.

4. Serve topped with the cilantro.

 SNACK

Fruit & Nut Butter

306 calories

2 bananas
1 tablespoon peanut butter

APPLE-CINNAMON
RICE PUDDING

Bananas
& Peanut
Butter

CHICKPEA & ROOT
VEGGIE BOWL

BOK CHOY MISO SOUP

M E A L
P R E P
for the rest of the week

Make the Potato Bake

Makes 2 servings

¾ cup cashews, soaked in water
  (see page 29)
1 cup vegetable broth, or 1 cup
  water mixed with 1 teaspoon
  veggie bouillon paste
1 garlic clove, minced
Sea salt and ground black pepper,
  to taste
1 bell pepper, chopped
1 zucchini, thinly sliced
3 cups thinly sliced potatoes
1 green onion, chopped

1. Preheat the oven to 400°F/
200°C.

2. Blend the soaked cashews with
the broth, garlic, and salt and
pepper until smooth.

3. Combine the bell pepper,
zucchini, potatoes, and green
onion in a bowl, add the cashew
mix, and mix well.

4. Transfer everything to a deep
baking dish (if it's big enough,
you can skip the bowl and mix
everything in the dish directly).
Bake for 45 minutes.

5. Let cool and store in the fridge
(either in the same dish, with a lid,
or in an airtight container).

Bake the Root Veggie Mix (optional; see page 92)

If you didn't make all of the Baked
Root Veggie Mix on Day 14, make
the rest using the remaining
ingredients.

Cook the Yellow Lentil Mix

Makes 2 servings

1 tablespoon olive oil
1 large onion, chopped
1 garlic clove, minced
2½ cups vegetable broth, or
  2½ cups water mixed with
  2 teaspoons veggie bouillon
  paste
1 cup dried yellow lentils (no need
  to soak them)
1 celery stalk, chopped
¼ cup sliced almonds

1. Heat the olive oil in a pot over
high heat, add the onion and
garlic, and cook for 2 minutes.

2. Reduce the heat to medium
and add the broth, lentils, celery,
and almonds. Cook for 15 to
20 minutes. Stir well and add
more water if necessary.

3. Let cool and store in an airtight
container in the fridge.

Note: Lentils can be done in as little
as 5 to 10 minutes (depending on the
brand), but I always find them a little too
al dente when cooking them for such
a short time only. Cooking them for
20 minutes will give you a consistency
that comes close to cauliflower or potato
mash, which is ideal for the soup on
Day 20. If you prefer your lentils slightly
firmer, simply reduce the cooking time to
10 to 15 minutes.

YELLOW
LENTIL
MIX

POTATO
BAKE

Day 19

"All the people in your life are truly doing the best they can with what they have. People can only love you to the capacity that they are able to love themselves. They can only forgive and embrace you to the capacity that they are able to forgive and embrace themselves. They can only give you what they have the capacity to give. You may think that you deserve more, and you may be correct. But that means nothing if a person simply doesn't have the ability to give it to you."

—Lisa Nichols, motivational speaker and author

BREAKFAST

Coco Mango Froyo

454 calories

Prep time: 3 minutes

Total time: 3 minutes

1½ cups frozen mango chunks

½ cup unsweetened coconut yogurt

1 tablespoon maple syrup

2 kiwis

2 tablespoons cashews

1. Blend the mango chunks, coconut yogurt, and maple syrup in a blender until smooth.

2. Slice or dice the kiwis and mix them into the yogurt. Enjoy with the cashews on the side.

Notes:

1. You don't have to peel the kiwis—the skin is edible. It is nutrient-dense and it'll save you time.

2. Depending on the type of blender you use, you may need to add a little water.

LUNCH

Chickpea & Arugula Salad

676 calories

Prep time: 2 minutes

Total time: 2 minutes (add 2 to 3 minutes if you decide to reheat the chickpeas)

1½ cups Cooked Chickpeas (page 29)

1½ cups arugula

1 avocado, sliced or diced

6 cherry tomatoes

1 serving Coconut Bacon (page 92)

Juice of 1 lime

1. Toss together the chickpeas, arugula, avocado, tomatoes, and coconut bacon. Squeeze the lime juice on top.

SNACK

Veggies & Tahini

241 calories

1 bell pepper, sliced

1 carrot, sliced

2 tablespoons tahini

DINNER

Mushroom Rice Bowl

600 calories

Prep time: 2 minutes

Cook time: 5 minutes

Total time: 7 minutes

1 cup Cooked Sushi Rice (page 92)

1 cup shredded Swiss chard

1 cup sliced mixed mushrooms

¼ cup vegetable broth, or ¼ cup water mixed with 1 teaspoon veggie bouillon paste

2 tablespoons sliced almonds

2 tablespoons nutritional yeast

1 tablespoon olive oil

1. Place all of the ingredients in a pot and cook over medium to high heat for 5 minutes. Stir well.

COCO MANGO FROYO

Veggies & Tahini

CHICKPEA & ARUGULA SALAD

MUSHROOM RICE BOWL

Day 20

"Every time you are tempted to react in the same old way, ask if you want to be a prisoner of the past or a pioneer of the future."

—Deepak Chopra, integrative medicine expert and self-help guru

BREAKFAST

Chocolate Granola

552 calories

Prep time: 2 minutes
Total time: 2 minutes

½ cup vegan granola
½ cup unsweetened coconut yogurt
1 tablespoon cacao powder
1 tablespoon maple syrup
1 kiwi
½ cup blueberries
2 tablespoons walnuts

1. Combine all of the ingredients in a bowl and enjoy!

LUNCH

Potato Bake on a Bed of Arugula

493 calories

Prep time: 2 minutes
Cook time: 2 to 3 minutes
Total time: 4 to 5 minutes

1 serving Potato Bake (page 104)
1½ cups arugula

1. Reheat the potato bake and then serve on a bed of arugula.

SNACK

Fruit & Nuts

177 calories
1 apple
2 tablespoons walnuts

DINNER

Coconut-Lentil Soup

772 calories

Prep time: 3 minutes
Cook time: 5 minutes
Total time: 8 minutes

1 serving Baked Root Veggie Mix (page 92)
1 serving Yellow Lentil Mix (page 92)
½ cup canned full-fat coconut milk
Sea salt and ground black pepper, to taste
½ tablespoon pumpkin seeds

1. Blend the root veggie mix, lentils, and coconut milk in a blender until smooth.

2. Transfer to a small pot and cook over medium heat for 5 minutes. Stir well. Season with salt and pepper.

3. Serve topped with the pumpkin seeds.

CHOCOLATE GRANOLA

Apple & Walnuts

POTATO BAKE
ON A BED OF ARUGULA

COCONUT-LENTIL SOUP

Day 21

"We do not grow absolutely, chronologically. We grow sometimes in one dimension, and not in another; unevenly. We grow partially. We are relative. We are mature in one realm, childish in another. The past, present, and future mingle and pull us backward, forward, or fix us in the present. We are made up of layers, cells, constellations."

—Anaïs Nin, writer

BREAKFAST

Banana-Chocolate Shake

534 calories

Prep time: 3 minutes

Total time: 3 minutes

3 frozen bananas, cut into chunks

1 cup cashew milk

2 tablespoons cacao powder

1 tablespoon peanut butter

2 tablespoons unsweetened coconut flakes

1. Blend the bananas, cashew milk, cacao powder, and peanut butter in a blender until smooth.

2. Serve topped with the coconut flakes.

LUNCH

Yellow Lentil Bowl

701 calories

Prep time: 2 minutes

Total time: 2 minutes (add 2 to 3 minutes if you choose to reheat the lentils and veggies)

1 serving Baked Root Veggie Mix (page 92)

1 serving Yellow Lentil Mix (page 104)

1 cup arugula

½ avocado, sliced or diced

1. Combine all of the ingredients in a bowl and enjoy!

DINNER

Potato Bake & Swiss Chard

499 calories

Prep time: 2 minutes

Cook time: 2 to 3 minutes

Total time: 4 to 5 minutes

1 serving Potato Bake (page 104)

2 cups shredded Swiss chard

1. Reheat the potato bake with the chard, and serve.

SNACK

Veggies & Tahini

253 calories

3 carrots, sliced

2 tablespoons tahini

BANANA-CHOCOLATE SHAKE

Carrots &
Tahini

POTATO BAKE & SWISS CHARD

YELLOW LENTIL
BOWL

End of Week Three:

JOURNALING EXERCISE

What was the best thing about this week?

....

What did I learn about myself this week?

....

What did I learn about my eating
habits this week?

....

What am I proudest of this week?

....

What could I improve next week?

....

What is my number-one goal for
next week?

Week Four
SHOPPING LIST

Note: You may already have some of the staple items listed, as they were used in previous weeks, so make sure you check your pantry before shopping.

FRUITS

Lemons	7
Papayas	3
Bananas	9
Pears	3
Berries, any kind (or use frozen mixed berries)	1 pint
Blueberries	1 pint
Avocados	2
Strawberries	1 quart
Lime	1
Raspberries	1 pint

Note: Feel free to get only one kind of berries if doing so will save money.

DRIED FRUIT

Unsweetened dried cranberries (or raisins)	1 package
Sun-dried tomatoes	1 package

VEGETABLES

Beets	3
Butternut squash	1
Shiitake mushrooms	6 ounces
Garlic	1 bulb
Cauliflower (you can cook and freeze any left over)	1 head
Kale	1 bunch
Fresh ginger	1 root
Celery	1 head
Red bell peppers	2
Potatoes	2
Zucchini	2
Brussels sprouts	9 ounces (1½ cups)
Broccoli (you can cook and freeze any left over)	1 head
Mesclun	1 bag (6 cups)
Mushrooms	9 ounces (3 cups)
Hearts of palm* (or artichokes)	1 jar (you'll need 1 cup)

FRESH HERBS

Cilantro*	1 bunch

LEGUMES

Kidney beans	three 15-ounce cans or 1 pound (2 cups) dried
Chickpeas	two 15-ounce cans or 1 bag (2 cups) dried
Tempeh	one 8-ounce package
Adzuki beans	two 15-ounce cans or 8 ounces (1 cup) dried

NUTS & SEEDS

Cashews	11 ounces
Sunflower seed butter (or peanut or almond butter)	1 container
Pine nuts (or cashews)*	2 ounces
*Brazil nuts**	2 ounces
Chia seeds	4 ounces
Peanuts	1 ounce
Hemp seeds (or ground flaxseed)*	0.5 ounce
*Almonds**	2 ounces

GRAINS

Gluten-free pasta, any shape	1 package
Gluten-free spaghetti (or just use more of the same pasta)*	1 package
Red quinoa	6 ounces

CONDIMENTS & STAPLE FOODS

Sea salt	Ground black pepper
Olive oil	
Maple syrup	Crushed red pepper flakes*
Smoked salt*	
Ground turmeric	Vegetable broth or veggie bouillon paste
Nutritional yeast	
Mustard	Miso paste*
	Cacao powder

MYLK

Cashew milk	1 quart
Full-fat coconut milk (for cooking)	1 small (8-ounce) can

DAY 22

Breakfast Oatmeal with Papaya & Brazil Nuts

Lunch Beet Salad with Miso-Ginger Tempeh & Red Quinoa

Snack Veggies & Nut Butter

Dinner Creamy Butternut Noodles

DAY 23

Breakfast Berry Green Smoothie Bowl

Lunch Creamy Butternut & Mesclun Pasta Bowl

Snack Fruit

Dinner Kidney Bean Quinoa Bowl

DAY 24

Breakfast Chia-Peach-Vanilla Pudding

Lunch Tempeh Bowl

Snack Fruit

Dinner Bell Pepper Coco Turmeric Stew

DAY 25

Breakfast Blueberry-Chocolate Shake

Lunch Chickpea & Strawberry Salad

Snack Fruit

Dinner Tomato-Mushroom Spaghetti with Candied Pine Nuts

DAY 26

Breakfast Sunflower Seed & Berry Toasts

Lunch Heart of Palm & Kale Salad

Snack Fruit & Nuts

Dinner Creamy Zucchini Bake

DAY 27

Breakfast Banana-Nut Oatmeal with Maple Drizzle

Lunch Hearts of Palm & Chickpea Sandwich

Snack Fruit & Nut Butter

Dinner Creamy Zucchini Bake with Potato Wedges

DAY 28

Breakfast Chocolate-Chia-Raspberry Pudding

Lunch Potato Bean Bowl

Snack Fruit

Dinner Butternut Bowl

Week Four

MENU

Day
21 MEAL
PREP

Cook the Kidney Beans (if using dried)

You'll need 2 cups cooked kidney beans. If using canned, you'll need 2 cans, no preparation needed. If starting with dried, cook ⅔ cup beans as described on page 29. Let cool and then store in an airtight container in the refrigerator.

Cook the Chickpeas (if using dried)

Since these are used on Day 25, I recommend using canned chickpeas (1 can). If you do use dried, cook ⅓ cup chickpeas as described on page 29 to make 1 cup cooked. Let cool and then store in an airtight container in the refrigerator.

Make the Baked Beets & Baked Butternut Squash

3 medium to large beets, peeled and diced (about 2 cups diced)
½ butternut squash, peeled, seeded, and diced

1. Preheat the oven to 400°F/ 200°C and line two baking sheets with parchment paper. Spread the beets on one baking sheet and the squash on the other.

2. Bake the beets and squash for 40 minutes. Let cool. Store 1½ cups beets in an airtight container in the fridge for later, and set aside the other ½ cup beets and the squash.

Note: Peeling the squash is optional; if it is organic, you can leave the skin on.

Bake the Shiitake Bacon

You can add the shiitake mushrooms to the oven while the beets and squash are baking to save time. Just don't forget to remove them after 20 minutes.

Makes 2 servings

2 cups sliced shiitake mushrooms
1 tablespoon olive oil
½ teaspoon sea salt or smoked salt

1. Preheat the oven to 400°F/ 200°C and line a baking sheet with parchment paper.

2. Toss together the mushrooms, oil, and salt. Bake for 20 minutes.

3. Let cool and store in an airtight container in the fridge.

Cook the Red Quinoa

You will need 3 cups cooked quinoa. Cook 1 cup quinoa as described on page 29. Let cool and then store in an airtight container in the fridge.

· CONTINUES ·

COOKED CAULIFLOWER & KALE MIX

Shiitake Bacon

BAKED BEETS

SUNFLOWER SEED, BEET & LEMON DRESSING

COOKED CHICKPEAS

MISO-GINGER TEMPEH

Creamy Butternut Sauce

COOKED KIDNEY BEANS

FROZEN BANANAS

COOKED RED QUINOA

BAKED BUTTERNUT SQUASH

Make the Cooked Cauliflower & Kale Mix

Makes 3 servings

1 tablespoon olive oil
3 cups chopped cauliflower
2 garlic cloves, minced
½ teaspoon sea salt
6 cups shredded kale

1. In a large pan, heat the olive oil over medium heat. Add the cauliflower, garlic, and salt and cook for 6 minutes. Add the kale to the pan and cook for an additional 2 minutes.

2. Let cool and store in an airtight container in the fridge.

Cook the Miso-Ginger Tempeh

Makes 2 servings

8 ounces tempeh, diced
1 garlic clove, minced
1 tablespoon olive oil
2 tablespoons grated fresh ginger
1 tablespoon miso paste
Pinch of sea salt (optional; see Note)

1. In a pan, cook the tempeh and garlic in the oil over medium heat for 3 minutes. Add the ginger, miso, and salt, if using, to the pan. Cook for another 3 to 4 minutes, mixing well.

2. Let cool and store in an airtight container in the fridge.

Note: The salt is optional, depending on which kind of miso you use; the miso may already be salty enough.

Make the Creamy Butternut Sauce

Makes 2 servings

Baked Butternut Squash (page 116)
½ cup cashews, soaked in water (see page 29)
½ celery stalk
¼ red bell pepper
4 tablespoons nutritional yeast
1 tablespoon cornstarch (optional)
Juice of 1 lemon
2 teaspoons mustard
1 teaspoon smoked paprika
½ teaspoon sea salt

1. Blend all of the ingredients in a blender until smooth and store in an airtight container in the fridge.

Make the Sunflower Seed, Beet & Lemon Dressing

Makes 2 servings

½ cup Baked Beets (page 116)
⅓ cup water
3 tablespoons sunflower seed
    butter
Juice of 1 lemon
Pinch of sea salt

1. Blend all of the ingredients in a blender until smooth. Store in an airtight container in the fridge.

Prep the Fruits & Veggies

Feel free to cut the veggies for the snacks in advance. It's always best to cut them the day of, but if you know you won't have enough time, prepare them and store them in an airtight container in the refrigerator. Freeze 4 of the bananas.

WEEK
4

Day 22

"Someone I loved once gave me a box full of darkness. It took me years to understand that this too, was a gift."

—Mary Oliver, American poet

SNACK

Veggies & Nut Butter

112 calories

2 celery stalks

1 tablespoon sunflower seed butter

BREAKFAST

Oatmeal with Papaya & Brazil Nuts

562 calories

Prep time: 2 minutes

Cook time: 2 minutes

Total time: 4 minutes

¾ cup quick oats

1¼ cups water

½ papaya, diced

¼ cup cashew milk

2 tablespoons sunflower seed butter

2 brazil nuts, chopped

2 teaspoons maple syrup

½ teaspoon vanilla extract (optional)

1. Cook the oats in a small pot with the water over high heat for 1½ to 2 minutes. Stir well.

2. Mix the cooked oats with all of the remaining ingredients and enjoy!

Note: You can also add the cashew milk directly to the pot with the water when cooking the oats.

LUNCH

Beet Salad with Miso-Ginger Tempeh & Red Quinoa

678 calories

Prep time: 2 minutes

Total time: 2 minutes (add 2 to 3 minutes if you choose to reheat the beets and tempeh)

1½ servings Baked Beets (page 116)

1 serving Miso-Ginger Tempeh (page 118)

½ cup Cooked Red Quinoa (page 116)

1 serving Cooked Cauliflower & Kale Mix (page 118)

1 serving Sunflower Seed, Beet & Lemon Dressing (page 119)

1. Combine the beets, tempeh, quinoa, and cauliflower-kale mix in a bowl, drizzle with the dressing, and enjoy!

DINNER

Creamy Butternut Noodles

639 calories

Prep time: 2 minutes

Cook time: 5 to 8 minutes

Total time: 7 to 10 minutes

6 ounces regular or gluten-free dried pasta

1 serving Creamy Butternut Sauce (page 118)

2 cups shredded kale

1. Cook the pasta according to the package instructions (this usually takes 3 to 6 minutes depending on which brand you use).

2. Drain the pasta. Divide the cooked pasta in half and reserve half for tomorrow (see Note).

3. Add the remaining pasta to a pan along with the sauce and kale. Cook over medium heat for 2 minutes and then serve.

Note: Here you cook twice as much pasta as you need, since you'll need it tomorrow as well. Keep the additional pasta in an airtight container in the refrigerator.

OATMEAL
WITH PAPAYA
& BRAZIL
NUTS

Celery &
Sunflower Seed
Butter

BEET SALAD WITH MISO-GINGER TEMPEH & RED QUINOA

CREAMY
BUTTERNUT
NOODLES

Day 23

"That's what it takes to get what you want. Not big scary leaps once a year. It takes small, but irritating moves every single day."

—Mel Robbins, life coach and motivational speaker

WEEK 4

BREAKFAST

Berry Green Smoothie Bowl

540 calories

Prep time: 3 minutes

Total time: 3 minutes

Smoothie Base
2 frozen bananas
1 ripe banana
1 cup shredded kale
½ cup cashew milk
½ teaspoon vanilla extract

Toppings
2 tablespoons almonds
1 tablespoon dried cranberries
¼ cup mixed berries (blueberries or raspberries)

1. Blend all the smoothie base ingredients in a blender until smooth.

2. Pour into a bowl, add the toppings, and enjoy!

LUNCH

Creamy Butternut & Mesclun Pasta Bowl

666 calories

Prep time: 2 minutes

Total time: 2 minutes (add 2 to 3 minutes if you choose to reheat the pasta and sauce)

Cooked regular or gluten-free pasta (from Day 22; see page 120)
1 serving Creamy Butternut Sauce (page 118)
1 cup mesclun lettuce

1. Combine all of the ingredients in a bowl and enjoy!

SNACK

Fruit & Nuts

123 calories

¼ cup unsweetened dried cranberries
2 tablespoons cashews

DINNER

Kidney Bean Quinoa Bowl

639 calories

Prep time: 2 minutes

Total time: 2 minutes (add 2 to 3 minutes if you choose to reheat the beans, cauliflower-kale mix, and quinoa)

1 cup Cooked Kidney Beans (page 116)
1 serving Cooked Cauliflower & Kale Mix (page 118)
1 cup Cooked Red Quinoa (page 116)
1 serving Sunflower Seed, Beet & Lemon Dressing (page 119)
1 serving Shiitake Bacon (page 116)

1. Combine all of the ingredients in a bowl and enjoy!

Prepare the Chia Pudding for Tomorrow

1¼ cups cashew milk
6 tablespoons chia seeds
1 tablespoon maple syrup
1 teaspoon vanilla extract

1. Mix the cashew milk, chia seeds, maple syrup, and vanilla in a glass or jar and store in the fridge overnight.

BERRY GREEN
SMOOTHIE
BOWL

*Dried
Cranberries &
Cashews*

CREAMY BUTTERNUT & MESCLUN PASTA BOWL

KIDNEY
BEAN
QUINOA
BOWL

Day 24

"Filtering the people we allow into our lives is probably the most important factor in determining whether we will live a happy life or not."

—James Altucher, entrepreneur and author

BREAKFAST

Chia-Pear-Vanilla Pudding

579 calories

Prep time: 2 minutes
Total time: 2 minutes

Chia Pudding (from last night; page 122)
1 ripe pear, chopped
3 tablespoons cashews, chopped

1. Top the chia pudding with the chopped pear and cashews and enjoy.

SNACK

Fruit & Nuts

113 calories

½ cup mixed berries
2 tablespoons almonds

LUNCH

Tempeh Bowl

663 calories

Prep time: 2 minutes
Total time: 2 minutes (add 2 to 3 minutes if you choose to reheat the beans and tempeh)

2 cups mesclun
1 cup Cooked Kidney Beans (page 116)
1 serving Miso-Ginger Tempeh (page 118)
3 tablespoons mustard

1. Combine all of the ingredients in a bowl and enjoy!

DINNER

Bell Pepper Coco Turmeric Stew

630 calories

Prep time: 2 minutes
Cook time: 7 minutes
Total time: 9 minutes

1 red bell pepper, sliced
1 garlic clove, minced
1 teaspoon olive oil
¾ cup vegetable broth, or ¾ cup water mixed with ¾ teaspoon veggie bouillon paste
1 cup canned full-fat coconut milk
½ cup Cooked Red Quinoa (page 116)
1 serving Cooked Cauliflower & Kale Mix (page 118)
2 teaspoons ground turmeric
Pinch of sea salt
½ handful of fresh herbs of your choice, for garnish (optional)

1. In a pot, sauté the bell pepper and garlic in the oil over high heat for 2 minutes.

2. Reduce the heat to medium and add the broth, coconut milk, quinoa, veggie mix, turmeric, and salt. Stir well and cook for 5 more minutes.

3. Serve topped with the herbs, if using.

CHIA-PEAR-
VANILLA
PUDDING

*Berries &
Almonds*

BELL PEPPER COCO TURMERIC STEW

TEMPEH BOWL

Day 25

"Forgive them. All of your thems. The more thems you can forgive, the lighter you'll feel."

—Karen Salmansohn, best-selling author

BREAKFAST

Blueberry-Chocolate Shake

565 calories

Prep time: 3 minutes
Total time: 3 minutes

2 frozen bananas
1 ripe banana
1½ cups cashew milk
½ cup frozen blueberries (or fresh)
2 tablespoons cacao powder
1 tablespoon sunflower seed butter
½ teaspoon vanilla extract

1. Blend all of the ingredients in a blender until smooth and enjoy!

SNACK

Fruit

117 calories

2 pears

LUNCH

Chickpea & Strawberry Salad

650 calories

Prep time: 5 minutes
Total time: 5 minutes

1 avocado, mashed
Juice of 1 lemon
Pinch of sea salt
Pinch of smoked salt (optional)
2 cups mesclun lettuce
1 cup strawberries, halved
1 cup Cooked Chickpeas (page 116)
Handful of fresh cilantro leaves

1. In a large bowl, mix together the mashed avocado, lemon juice, sea salt, and smoked salt, if using, then "massage" it into the mesclun.

2. Mix in the strawberries, chickpeas, and cilantro and enjoy!

DINNER

Tomato-Mushroom Spaghetti with Candied Pine Nuts

571 calories

Prep time: 2 minutes
Cook time: 7 to 8 minutes
Total time: 9 to 10 minutes

3 ounces regular or gluten-free dried spaghetti
1 tablespoon olive oil
1 cup sliced mushrooms
1 garlic clove, minced
3 tablespoons pine nuts
1 tablespoon maple syrup
5 sun-dried tomatoes, if possible salt-free, chopped if large
Pinch of sea salt (see Note)
Pinch of ground black pepper
Handful of fresh basil leaves (optional)

1. Cook the spaghetti according to the package instructions (3 to 8 minutes, depending on the brand).

2. Meanwhile, heat the oil in a pan over medium heat and sauté the mushrooms and garlic for 5 minutes.

3. Mix the pine nuts with the maple syrup. Add the pine nuts and tomatoes to the pan. Season with salt and pepper and cook for another 2 minutes.

4. Toss the pasta with the mushroom-tomato mixture and garnish with the basil, if using.

Note: If you can't find unsalted tomatoes, omit the salt in this recipe.

BLUEBERRY-CHOCOLATE
SHAKE

Chickpea &
Strawberry Salad

PEARS

TOMATO-MUSHROOM
SPAGHETTI WITH CANDIED
PINE NUTS

M E A L
P R E P

for the rest of the week

Cook the Adzuki Beans (if using dried)

If using canned, you'll need 2 cans, no preparation needed. If starting with dried, cook ⅔ cup beans as described on page 29 to make 2 cups. Let cool and refrigerate in an airtight container.

Cook the Chickpeas (if using dried)

If using canned, you'll need 1 can, no preparation needed. If starting with dried, cook ⅓ cup chickpeas as described on page 29 to make 1 cup. Let cool and refrigerate in an airtight container.

Make the Creamy Cilantro Dressing

Makes 2 servings

Handful of fresh cilantro leaves
¼ cup pine nuts
¼ cup water
Juice of 1 lemon
1 garlic clove, peeled
½ teaspoon sea salt

1. Blend all of the ingredients in a blender until smooth.

2. Store in an airtight container in the fridge.

Make the Baked Butternut Squash & Baked Potato Wedges

This will make 2 servings of baked butternut squash and 2 servings of baked potato wedges.

½ butternut squash, seeds removed, diced (about 2 cups)
2 medium potatoes, cut into wedges (about 2 cups)
2 teaspoons olive oil
½ teaspoon sea salt

1. Preheat the oven to 400°F/ 200°C. Line two baking sheets with parchment paper.

2. Spread the squash on one baking sheet and the potatoes on the other.

3. Drizzle the olive oil on top of the potatoes and sprinkle the salt on top.

4. Bake the squash and potatoes for 45 minutes.

5. Let cool and store, separately, in airtight containers in the fridge.

Make the Zucchini Bake

Makes 2 servings

You can bake this at the same time as the root vegetables, on a separate baking sheet.

2 zucchini, thinly sliced
1 cup cashews, soaked in water (see page 29)
⅔ cup vegetable broth, or ⅔ cup water mixed with ¾ teaspoon veggie bouillon paste
Juice of 1 lemon
4 tablespoons nutritional yeast
1 garlic clove, peeled
1 teaspoon smoked paprika
½ teaspoon sea salt
Pinch of ground black pepper

1. Preheat the oven to 400°F/ 200°C if needed (see note above). Place the zucchini on a small baking sheet.

2. Blend all the other ingredients in a blender until smooth. Pour over the zucchini.

3. Bake for 45 minutes.

4. Let cool and store in an airtight container in the fridge.

Make the Cooked Green Veggie Mix

Makes 2 servings

1½ cups halved Brussels sprouts
1½ cups chopped broccoli
½ teaspoon sea salt
1 tablespoon olive oil

1. Sauté the vegetables with the salt in the oil over medium heat for 7 minutes. Let cool and store in an airtight container in the fridge.

COOKED GREEN VEGGIE MIX

COOKED ADZUKI BEANS

COOKED CHICKPEAS

BAKED BUTTERNUT SQUASH & BAKED POTATO WEDGES

Creamy Cilantro
Dressing

ZUCCHINI BAKE

Day 26

"The universe buries strange jewels deep within us all, and then stands back to see if we can find them."
—Elizabeth Gilbert, author

WEEK 4

BREAKFAST

Sunflower Seed & Berry Toasts

576 calories

Prep time: 2 minutes
Total time: 2 minutes

2 slices regular or gluten-free bread
3 tablespoons sunflower seed butter
½ cup fresh strawberries, halved
1 glass (1½ cups) cold cashew milk

1. Toast the bread (optional) and top with the sunflower seed butter and berries.

2. Enjoy with a glass of ice-cold cashew milk.

LUNCH

Heart of Palm & Kale Salad

585 calories

Prep time: 3 minutes
Total time: 3 minutes

1 serving Creamy Cilantro Dressing (page 128)
2 cups shredded kale
1 serving Baked Butternut Squash (page 128)
½ cup cherry tomatoes, halved
½ jar hearts of palm, cut into ½-inch slices
2 slices regular or gluten-free bread, toasted and cut into croutons
1 tablespoon hemp seeds
2 tablespoons nutritional yeast

1. In a large bowl, massage the dressing into the kale.

2. Add the butternut squash, tomatoes, hearts of palm, croutons, and hemp seeds and toss together.

3. Sprinkle with the nutritional yeast and enjoy!

DINNER

Creamy Zucchini Bake

641 calories

Prep time: 0 minutes
Cook time: 4 minutes
Total time: 4 minutes

1 serving Zucchini Bake (page 128)
1 cup shredded kale
½ cup Cooked Adzuki Beans (page 128)

1. Reheat the zucchini bake with the kale and beans in a pot or pan over medium to high heat for 4 minutes, then enjoy!

SNACK

Fruit & Nuts

193 calories

2 papayas, sliced
Juice of 1 lime (squeezed over the papayas)
1 tablespoon sliced almonds

SUNFLOWER
SEED & BERRY
TOASTS

HEART OF PALM & KALE SALAD

CREAMY
ZUCCHINI
BAKE

Papaya &
Almonds

Day 27

1,990 CALORIES

"Nothing has transformed my life more than realizing that it's a waste of time to evaluate my worthiness by weighing the reaction of the people in the stands."

—Brené Brown, researcher, motivational speaker, and author

SNACK

Fruit & Nut Butter

309 calories

2 bananas

1 tablespoon sunflower seed butter

WEEK 4

BREAKFAST

Banana-Nut Oatmeal with Maple Drizzle

484 calories

Prep time: 1 minute
Cook time: 2 minutes
Total time: 3 minutes

½ cup quick-cooking oats
¾ cup water
½ cup cashew milk
½ teaspoon vanilla extract
1 banana, sliced
3 tablespoons chopped peanuts
1 tablespoon maple syrup

1. In a small pot, cook the oats in the water over high heat for 1½ to 2 minutes.

2. Add the cashew milk and vanilla and stir well.

3. Serve in a bowl and top with the banana, peanuts, and maple syrup.

LUNCH

Hearts of Palm & Chickpea Sandwich

589 calories

Prep time: 3 minutes
Total time: 3 minutes

1 cup Cooked Chickpeas (page 128)
½ jar hearts of palm, chopped
Juice of 1 lemon
1 teaspoon olive oil
Pinch of sea salt
Pinch of smoked paprika
2 slices regular or gluten-free bread, toasted
Handful of mesclun lettuce
2 tablespoons mustard (optional)

1. In a bowl, mash the chickpeas, hearts of palm, lemon juice, oil, salt, and smoked paprika using a fork (or use a food processor).

2. Spread on top of the toasts and sandwich with the mesclun and the mustard, if using.

DINNER

Creamy Zucchini Casserole with Potato Wedges

608 calories

Prep time: 0 minutes
Cook time: 4 minutes
Total time: 4 minutes

1 serving Creamy Zucchini Bake (page 130)
1 serving Baked Potato Wedges (page 128)
1 cup mixed greens

1. Reheat the zucchini bake for 4 minutes (you can reheat the wedges at the same time). Serve with the greens and enjoy!

Prepare the Chia Pudding for Tomorrow

¾ cup cashew milk
6 tablespoons chia seeds
2 tablespoons cacao powder
2 teaspoons maple syrup
1 teaspoon vanilla extract

1. Mix the cashew milk, chia seeds, cacao, maple syrup, and vanilla in a glass or jar and store in the fridge overnight.

HEARTS OF PALM & CHICKPEA SANDWICH

BANANA-NUT OATMEAL WITH MAPLE DRIZZLE

Bananas & Sunflower Seed Butter

CREAMY ZUCCHINI CASSEROLE WITH POTATO WEDGES

Day 28

"Do the best you can until you know better. Then when you know better, do better."

—Maya Angelou, American poet and activist

WEEK
4

BREAKFAST

Chocolate-Chia-Raspberry Pudding

559 calories

Prep time: 2 minutes
Total time: 2 minutes

Chia Pudding (from Day 27; see page 132)
½ cup fresh raspberries (see Note)
2 tablespoons chopped cashews

1. Top the chia pudding with the raspberries and cashews and enjoy!

Note: You can use frozen berries; heat them in a small pot for 2 to 3 minutes beforehand.

SNACK

Fruit

70 calories

1 cup mixed berries

LUNCH

Potato Bean Bowl

740 calories

Prep time: 3 minutes
Total time: 3 minutes (add 2 to 3 minutes if you choose to reheat the beans and potatoes)

1 avocado, mashed
Juice of 1 lemon
Pinch of smoked salt
Pinch of ground black pepper
1 cup Cooked Adzuki Beans (page 128)
1 serving Cooked Green Veggie Mix (page 128)
1 serving Baked Potato Wedges (page 128)
⅓ cup cherry tomatoes, halved
Handful of fresh cilantro leaves

1. In a large bowl, mix the avocado with the lemon juice, salt, and pepper. Add all of the remaining ingredients and serve.

DINNER

Butternut Bowl

571 calories

Prep time: 2 minutes
Total time: 2 minutes (add 2 to 3 minutes if you choose to reheat the butternut squash and beans)

1 serving Baked Butternut Squash (page 128)
1 serving Cooked Green Veggie Mix (page 128)
1 cup Cooked Adzuki Beans (page 128)
1 serving Creamy Cilantro Dressing (page 128)

1. Combine all of the ingredients in a bowl and enjoy!

CHOCOLATE-CHIA-
RASPBERRY PUDDING

Berries

POTATO BEAN BOWL

BUTTERNUT
BOWL

After the Vegan Reset

JOURNALING EXERCISE

In the form of a journal entry or a letter, write down what you believe you accomplished and improved over the past four weeks, how you feel now, and which of these qualities you plan to continue to grow. Then, write down what areas you struggled with the most and what actions you will implement to work on these challenges in the future.

Part

THREE

Beyond the Reset:

Continuing with a Vegan Lifestyle

ONCE YOU'VE COMPLETED the 28-day reset, you might want to continue eating vegan and learning more about a vegan lifestyle. Veganism has become one of the fastest growing "trends" in the past few years in many different countries all over the world, but many people are still confused about what veganism actually is and are unaware of the reasons why some choose to make such a seemingly drastic lifestyle change. The word "vegan" refers to the ethical decision to no longer consume or use any animal products or by-products, as well as products tested on animals, in an attempt to reduce and eliminate animal suffering. (If you are already a vegan, you still might find some of the information and tips in this section useful, or you can skip ahead to find some additional recipes starting on page 154.)

From an early age, we're taught that eating meat is normal and necessary, and we go through life thinking of ourselves as omnivores or even carnivores, so much so that meat and dairy consumption is an integral part of our culture.

If you compare the anatomy of human beings with that of non-human animals, our anatomy is actually surprisingly similar to that of herbivores and frugivores (fruit eaters). The stomachs of true carnivores are much more acidic and their digestive tracts much shorter than those of herbivores and human beings. Animal protein contains no fiber, making it very difficult to digest. In practice, this means that while fruits and vegetables only take a few hours to digest, meat can take up to three days. The bodies of true carnivores are designed to make this process as efficient and quick as possible—ours aren't. That being said, it is undeniable that at one point in our evolution, human beings resorted to cooking and eating meat for sustenance. But that doesn't mean that we still have to rely on meat in this day and age. Here are some of the main reasons to go vegan.

"Factory farm: a large industrialized farm; especially: a farm on which large numbers of livestock are raised indoors in conditions intended to maximize production at minimal cost."
—Merriam-Webster's Dictionary

ETHICS

Because we have the physical ability to digest meat, many think that we are omnivores, but the answer isn't quite so simple. Yes, we are *capable* of eating practically anything in order to survive, but we have no biological need for animal products. In fact, the overconsumption of processed meats and other animal products has actually been linked to numerous illnesses, including cardiovascular diseases.

Veganism isn't about debunking everything we've ever been taught, but rather about critically examining the information that we use to justify our consumption of other sentient beings. There is a reason slaughterhouses don't have glass walls. I think that, deep down, we already know that there is something horrific about killing animals. On top of that, commercial animal agriculture is both cruel and unsustainable.

The day I came across the book *Eating Animals* by Jonathan Safran Foer, which was the first book that introduced me to the reality of factory farms, I read the first page and instantly knew I was not going to like what I read. So instead of continuing, I closed the book and decided that I wasn't ready for it. It took me a few months before I finally had the courage to keep reading. We have no biological need for animal products and, therefore, if given the choice between compassion and unnecessary suffering, our choice should be an obvious one. I want to emphasize that my goal is not to depict meat eaters as evil people. People eat meat because they've been taught that it is necessary and normal. I ate meat for most of my life and I don't think that I was a bad person. This is not about attacking anyone or feeling superior. For me, it's about making kinder, more compassionate decisions.

This can be a very sensitive topic, because how do you condemn an action without condemning those who are, often unknowingly, responsible for it? You do so by focusing on the victims—the animals—first and foremost and by meeting people where they are, encouraging every step toward a kinder lifestyle with patience and compassion. So, if you are still eating meat, I'm not here to judge you, but rather to show you all the wonderful things veganism has to offer.

Is Vegetarianism Not Enough?

To someone hearing about veganism for the first time, cutting out *all* animal products may seem extreme. Would it not be enough to just be vegetarian? Before knowing anything about veganism, I had a vague idea of the meat industry and what animals had to endure before being killed for food. I knew that there were cases of cruelty against animals in some slaughterhouses and I had seen snippets of footage that undercover activists had secretly recorded. I was convinced, however, that the circumstances I had seen in those undercover videos were the exception, not the norm. I thought that most animals were treated "nicely" and that killing them was an unfortunate but necessary step.

As I started finding out more about the meat industry and then the dairy and egg industries, I realized that these circumstances were not only *not* the exception, they were also not even the worst-case scenario. The book that opened my eyes was Gail Eisnitz's *Slaughterhouse*. Gail went undercover for several years, exposing the gruesome conditions and uncountable cases of neglect she encountered. It was a passage from this book that ultimately made me go vegan. Factory farms are necessary in order to keep up with the incredibly high demand for animal products that exists today. In the United States alone, 10 billion land animals are raised and killed for food every year, the majority of them on factory farms, where the conditions are horrendously cruel.

So, are animal by-products that don't involve killing animals okay? Is there such a thing as ethical vegetarianism?

What many people don't know is that even the dairy and egg industries are responsible for killing billions of animals. The veal industry is a by-product of the dairy industry, for instance. Just like humans, cows need to be pregnant in order to produce milk. They are therefore artificially inseminated over and over again throughout their lives so that they produce milk constantly. After the calf is born, it is taken from its mother either to be killed and sold as meat or, if she is female, to become a dairy cow herself. When their bodies are no longer capable of producing milk quickly enough, they are then slaughtered and their meat sold to fast-food chains or similar facilities. The egg industry disposes of male chicks, since they aren't able to produce eggs. Vegetarianism is a step in the right direction, but veganism is the only way to reduce all animal suffering.

What About Organic, Free-Range & Cage-Free?

As conscious consumers, we deserve to know how the products and foods we buy are made. But we live in an imperfect world and things aren't all black and white. Labels like "free-range," "cage-free," "organic," "happy," or "humane" are meant to make the consumer feel more at ease. But what do these labels really mean? "Cage-free," for instance, literally only means that animals like chickens are not held in a cage. That doesn't mean access to the outdoors, daylight, or enough space to spread their wings. I don't doubt that some farmers genuinely care for the animals they raise. Even under the best conditions, though, we should question whether it is ethical to keep animals in captivity, and kill them, for profit. Or, alternatively, to question whether animals have the same worth and value as humans.

The questions we should really be asking ourselves are "Do they feel pain?" (they do); "Is eating them necessary for us to survive?" (it's not); and "Would I want to live like that?" (would you?).

"People eat meat and think they will become strong as an ox, forgetting that the ox eats grass."
—Pino Caruso

THE ENVIRONMENT

Another reason to go vegan that affects all of us, without exception, is the impact that animal agriculture has on the environment. Animal agriculture, especially the mass production of animal products, is so unsustainable that if we don't take action soon, the consequences will be devastating. Growing animals for food requires so many resources, including water and grains, that it would be more sustainable, affordable, and logical to simply feed these resources to humans directly. Furthermore, animal agriculture creates such a large amount of waste that it is responsible for more greenhouse gas emissions than all means of transportation combined, making it one of the main causes of climate change. The documentary *Cowspiracy* explores this in detail.

In an effort to be more environmentally friendly and save the planet, we're told to reduce our water consumption, drive hybrid cars, and recycle. Here are some notable facts outlined in *Cowspiracy*:

- Animal agriculture is responsible for 18 percent of greenhouse gas emissions, more than the combined exhaust from all transportation.

- Livestock and their by-products account for at least 32,000 million tons of carbon dioxide (CO_2) per year, or 51 percent of all worldwide greenhouse gas emissions.

- Cows produce 150 billion gallons of methane per day; methane is more harmful to the atmosphere than carbon dioxide.

- 2,500 gallons of water are needed to produce 1 pound of beef. Agriculture is responsible for 80 to 90 percent of U.S. water consumption.

- Livestock or livestock feed occupies one-third of the earth's ice-free land.

- Three-quarters of the world's fisheries are exploited or depleted. We could see fishless oceans by 2048.

- Scientists estimate that as many as 650,000 whales, dolphins, and seals are killed every year by fishing vessels.

- Animal agriculture is responsible for up to 91 percent of Amazon rain forest destruction.

- Worldwide, at least 50 percent of grain is fed to livestock.

- Each day, a person who eats a vegan diet saves 1,100 gallons of water, 45 pounds of grain, 30 square feet of forested land, 20 pounds carbon dioxide equivalent, and one animal's life.

HEALTH BENEFITS

The word "vegan" itself refers to ethics and encompasses other lifestyle changes to support the ethical treatment of animals (more on that on page 141). But a person can adopt a plant-based diet for health reasons without necessarily changing their entire lifestyle.

Switching to a whole foods plant-based diet can make you feel incredible, especially if you're used to eating highly processed foods. The more fresh fruits and vegetables, legumes, starches, herbs, and other nutrient-dense plants you consume, the better you're likely to feel. Plants are rich in fiber and contain no cholesterol, significantly improving your digestion and reducing your risk of cardiovascular diseases. Switching to a plant-based diet has been shown to halt and even reverse conditions such as type 2 diabetes, heart disease, and obesity. That is why many people choose to adopt a plant-based diet even if their motivation is neither ethical nor environmental.

There is no one-size-fits-all diet

The beauty of the human body is that we are able to thrive on a variety of foods and that we can adapt to so many different climates and living conditions. Many diets will promise you that their way is *the* right and often the *only* way to eat. Most of them work temporarily because they follow the very simple concept of making you consume fewer calories than you burn, which, while effective in the short run, is not necessarily sustainable in the long run. *Vegan Reset* is here to give you tools that you can incorporate well beyond the 28-day program, since only long-term changes will bring about long-lasting results. Some people do better with a little more fat and protein in their diets and others feel great eating primarily carbohydrates, which is absolutely fine. My goal is to show you how you can find the macronutrients and micronutrients you need from plants and make this lifestyle work for you.

Don't think of the word "diet" as a short-term, restrictive way to eat; its etymology is a word for "way of living." So we can think of a "diet" as any sustainable way to incorporate healthy habits that will allow you to live a happier life in the long run. Accepting that there isn't *one* diet that works for everyone allows for much more flexibility and room to experiment. There are many ways to eat within the vegan lifestyle. When I say that there is no one-size-fits-all diet, I don't mean that not everyone can go vegan, but rather that it is important to find the diet that works best for you within the vegan lifestyle.

Veganism is amazing, but it's not a magic pill

Veganism can have amazing benefits, but it should not be confused with a magic pill that will cure you of anything, nor does it have to be. Claiming that veganism is the solution to everything can be perceived as both dogmatic and even dangerous. Your goal should be to feel healthy and happy while eating in a way that aligns with your ethical values and supports your well-being.

There is more than one plant-based diet

Veganism isn't automatically healthy. You can be vegan and eat veggie burgers, pizza, and chocolate all day. The healthiest plant-based diets are those that include an abundance of fresh produce and unprocessed staple foods, but including a small amount of processed vegan foods is absolutely fine.

"The question is not can they reason nor can they talk but can they suffer?"
—Jeremy Bentham

What does it mean to be vegan?

While many believe that veganism is just about the food we eat, it is actually an entire lifestyle that seeks to end animal exploitation in everything we do. The line between "vegan" and "plant-based" is often a blurry one when it comes to people's understanding of the concept of veganism. To make this line a little less blurry, here is a bit more information about the different categories of vegetarianism and veganism that exist.

Pescatarian

People who identify as pescatarian eat no animal flesh except for fish. But even though they live in the water, fish feel pain just like other animals do and can be very sophisticated and intelligent beings. Pescatarianism can be a step toward veganism, but eating fish is no more ethical than eating the flesh of other animals.

Vegetarian (Lacto-Ovo & Lacto)

Vegetarianism is commonly understood as not eating any meat, including fish. Within that category, there are lacto-ovo vegetarians, who still eat dairy products and eggs, and lacto-vegetarians who eat dairy products but no meat and no eggs.

Plant-Based

"Plant-based" means eating a primarily vegan diet while not necessarily changing one's entire lifestyle. Some people who eat a plant-based diet might consume a very small percentage of animal products, like honey or the occasional egg. People who eat a plant-based diet as opposed to a vegan one usually do so for health reasons rather than ethical concerns. Why is the distinction here important? Because if a decision is an ethical one and we are driven by compassion, we are more likely to try and find ways to make it work long-term.

A Word About PROTEIN

We have become obsessed with protein, and many people immediately associate the absence of meat with protein deficiencies. We consume protein shakes and protein bars and fill our plates with lean meats and eggs so that we don't end up losing muscle mass and becoming deficient. I, too, used to be obsessed with it. I remember being so afraid of not consuming enough protein that I would drink liters of cow's milk throughout the day, and I would make sure that every meal included at least one source of protein, preferably chicken, fish, or cheese.

Beyond being obsessed with protein, we seem to believe that animals and their by-products are the only reliable source of it. We forget that the animals we eat for protein got *their* protein from plants. Plants actually contain plenty of protein, and the daily requirements for protein aren't nearly as high as we think they are, so getting sufficient protein from plant-based sources is relatively easy on a balanced plant-based diet.

Vegan

Veganism is a lifestyle that seeks to exclude all animal products in order to minimize the unnecessary suffering of animals. For many vegans, the health benefits of veganism are merely a bonus, but the main motivation is ethical. When we are so used to consuming and using animals and their by-products, it can seem overwhelming to suddenly exclude them. Something I recommend to both new vegans and non-vegans is taking a look at their pantries, fridges, and closets to take inventory. Even if your intention is not to go vegan immediately or at all, becoming aware of just how many of your belongings are derived from animals can be a very interesting and eye-opening exercise. The goal is not to make you feel guilty or ashamed, but just to make you become a little more aware. When taking a look at your current habits and at what is in your pantry and closet, here are all the non-vegan items to look out for.

Food

Meat and bones The flesh of all animals (beef, pork, chicken, lamb, fish, all seafood, and every other living being) as well as their bones, often found in broth or products containing gelatin. This includes anything flavored with meat or meat broth.

Dairy Milk (from a cow, a goat, or any other animal), cheese, yogurt, cream, ice cream, butter, and ghee. Many processed foods contain milk even when you wouldn't expect them to. Most brands of snack chips, for instance, contain small amounts of casein, the protein found in dairy. Also beware some vegetarian proteins or meat alternatives. Unless they're clearly labeled as vegan, they may still include some dairy and/or eggs. Milk chocolate almost always includes dairy, unless otherwise specified, but most dark chocolates are vegan. To be sure, check the ingredient list and look for words or phrases with "milk," "casein," or "lactose"/"lact-" in them.

Many foods, even though they don't list milk in the ingredient list, state that they *"may contain traces"* of it. That usually means that the factory that made them also makes foods that contain milk. They mention it for legal reasons in case of allergies, but, generally speaking, there is no need to worry about cross-contamination, and most vegans do consume these foods.

Eggs Eggs are found in most pastries, desserts, and some breakfast foods like pancakes and waffles, as well as some types of pasta, especially fresh pasta. Luckily, more and more vegan alternatives are becoming available, so finding egg-free products is not nearly as challenging as it used to be, and you can often substitute other ingredients, such as flaxseed or applesauce, for eggs when baking.

Honey Since honey is produced by bees, it is not considered vegan. The idea behind veganism is to avoid animal exploitation for human profit altogether, no matter how small the animal. Brown rice syrup, maple syrup, and coconut nectar are good plant-based alternatives.

Sugar Some refined sugar is processed with bone char, making it non-vegan. You can find out whether or not a certain brand uses that process by checking online, but the easiest way to make sure the sugar you consume is vegan is by opting for an organic brand.

Alcohol As with sugar, the only thing that would make certain wines and beers not vegan is the filtering process. Some brands use egg whites, gelatin, or isinglass (a kind of gelatin obtained from fish) to filter their alcohol. Websites and apps like Barnivore can help you find out whether or not a brand is vegan if it is not clearly indicated on the label. All beers that follow the German *Reinheitsgebot* (a regulation about the purity of beer that has been in existence since 1516 and that states that beer may only contain water, hops, and barley) are vegan by default.

BEYOND FOOD

As I've mentioned, veganism goes beyond the food we eat. It is difficult to fully grasp just how much of our daily lives includes products that are either directly or indirectly linked to animal exploitation. As you go through the list of things that include animal products, it is normal to start feeling slightly overwhelmed, but please remember that this is not about making you feel pressured. If the first step is becoming more aware and if that's all you're ready for right now, that's okay. One step at a time is all it takes to get started.

Clothes

Vegans don't wear leather, wool, fur, cashmere, silk, or any other type of animal skin or by-product. Although even before I went vegan I was opposed to wearing fur, I had plenty of leather bags and shoes, wool sweaters, and silk blouses. It's understandable if you can't immediately invest in a new wardrobe, so anything you bought before going vegan is technically okay to keep, but if you don't feel comfortable wearing these items anymore, you can recycle or donate them. Some of the best places to donate non-vegan clothes are animal sanctuaries and rescue shelters. These facilities use donated fur coats and wool items to keep rescued animals warm during the winter.

Cosmetics

There are cosmetic products that contain ingredients derived from animal products and cosmetic products that have been tested on animals. Neither are vegan, but it is important to make the distinction, because the "cruelty-free" label doesn't necessarily make a product vegan. Luckily, there are plenty of products we can rely on that don't involve or harm animals during their making. Since ingredient lists can be very confusing, it is easier to either look for products that are clearly labeled vegan or look for vegan and cruelty-free brands online before making a purchase. If you have doubts about the products you are currently using, you can simply email the brands' customer service and ask whether or not they are vegan.

Homemade Beauty/Skin-Care Products

High-quality skin and hair products that neither contain animal products nor have been tested on animals can be quite pricey (although there are, of course, exceptions), but you can make your own products with just a few basic ingredients. Of course, supporting ethical vegan companies is always a great idea, but it's also good to know that you can create some basic skin-care products at home.

Sea salt & olive oil scrub

Mix about ½ cup olive oil with ½ cup sea salt to make a great exfoliator for your body. While the salt exfoliates, the oil immediately rehydrates the skin, leaving soft and smooth results. Tip: Sea salt is a little too rough to be used on the face, so, for more sensitive skin, you can either substitute finer-grained salt or use the coffee and coconut oil scrub that follows.

Coffee & coconut oil scrub

Mix about 1 cup ground coffee with ½ cup sugar, ½ cup coconut oil (coconut oil hardens in lower temperatures, so make sure you melt it beforehand), and 2 teaspoons vanilla extract (optional; you could also use ground cinnamon or cacao powder). Apply the scrub to your skin with your hands or a wash cloth and rinse off with water.

Coconut oil moisturizer & makeup remover

Coconut oil is one of the best natural moisturizers. You've probably heard a lot about coconut oil in the past few years, and it's important to realize that much of the hype surrounding it is due to clever marketing strategies. It is, after all, a type of oil, and using any other oil like olive oil or argan oil will give you similar results. Coconut oil does, however, smell a bit better (or, if you choose refined coconut oil, it can be almost odorless). You can apply it to your skin as is and even use it as massage oil. It's also a great natural makeup remover. Apply a bit of it to an organic cotton ball or reusable washcloth, remove any traces of makeup, and then rinse with water.

Avocado face mask

Ripe avocados are a wonderful base for face masks. You can mash them (1 avocado is enough for one or two face masks) and use them by themselves or mix them with other ingredients, like: cooked oatmeal (make sure you let it cool before applying it), maple syrup, coconut yogurt, or lemon juice. Apply the mask for about 10 minutes and then remove it gently with a wet washcloth.

COFFEE SCRUB

Avocado face mask

CUCUMBER TONER
& FACE MASK

SEA SALT AND OLIVE OIL SCRUB

Baking soda

COCOA BUTTER

OLIVE OIL
HAIR MASK

Cucumber toner & face mask

If you have a juicer, you can use it to make toners and face masks. Alternatively, you can use a blender and then strain the mixture through a strainer or nut milk bag. Juice 1 or 2 cucumbers (with the skin) and then mix the juice with about ¼ cup apple cider vinegar to make a toner. Apply the toner to an organic cotton ball or reusable wash cloth to cleanse your skin, and then rinse with water. You can use the juice pulp to make a toning face mask by mixing it with the juice of 1 lemon or lime.

Olive oil hair mask

If you have particularly dry hair, olive oil or shea butter makes an extremely moisturizing hair mask. Massage the oil or butter into your hair (you can do this with dry or towel-dried hair) and let sit for 20 minutes to 1 hour depending on how much care your hair needs. Wash your hair to remove the oil. Note that you may need to shampoo and rinse a few times in order to get all of it out.

Baking soda deodorant

Baking soda is one of the best natural deodorants. Apply a bit of water to your armpits and then apply 1 to 2 teaspoons of baking soda. Since the skin is wet, it will stick naturally. It neutralizes smells and keeps you feeling fresh. If you prefer a creamy deodorant and/or want to add some scent, mix it with coconut oil and essential oils (lavender or grapefruit, for instance).

Cocoa butter lip balm

One of my absolute favorite ingredients is cocoa butter. You can make amazing vegan white chocolate with it (simply mix it with a bit of coconut oil and maple syrup and then let it harden in the fridge or freezer) or use it as lip balm. Either let it melt a little (be careful not to apply it when it's hot and not to melt it too much!) or mix it with a little coconut oil.

Body brush

Dry brushes are a great natural skin-care tool. You can get a body brush for $5 to $25 (and up) online, at drugstores, or at health stores. Just make sure your brush isn't made with animal hair/products. The skin is our biggest organ and we shed dead skin cells every day. To help the process, use your body brush for 3 to 5 minutes before you shower. You can do this every day, every other day, or just once a week (or whenever you feel like it). Start with your hands and feet and then make your way toward your heart; this is the best way to stimulate your blood circulation.

Household products

As with cosmetics, in order to be vegan, cleaning products should neither contain animal products nor have been tested on animals. Some fabric softeners, for instance, use animal grease as part of their ingredient list. Look for labels that indicate that the product is both cruelty-free and vegan. The good news is that many vegan brands often also seek to exclude harmful toxins and strive to be as eco-friendly as possible, thereby making the products safer for you and your family and kinder to the environment.

Entertainment

Since vegans are against every form of animal exploitation, this includes the use of animals for our entertainment, such as in zoos, rodeos, and circuses. No animal belongs in captivity, but the suffering of wild animals trained to perform tricks is particularly immense. In the wild, these animals often roam for many miles, but in captivity, they're confined to small cages and are chained, keeping them from moving freely. Trainers often resort to cruel and violent punishments in order to make animals like elephants and lions perform tricks. A wonderful alternative is to visit farm sanctuaries where animals are being looked after rather than looked at.

Socializing as a vegan

Eating out as a vegan can sometimes be a little challenging, but if you plan ahead and consider these tips and tricks, you'll be able to find vegan options almost anywhere you go.

If you can, opt for a restaurant that features at least some vegan options, like a fully vegan, vegetarian, or vegan-friendly restaurant. You can find lists on websites and apps like Happy Cow, or simply google "vegan restaurant" followed by the name of the city or area you're in. If you can't find any restaurants that specifically cater to vegans, or you don't get to choose the restaurant, there are still ways to make it work. If you know which restaurant you'll be going to ahead of time, look up the menu to see if they offer any vegan options or if any of their dishes can easily be veganized. Restaurants are used to people asking for adjustments and many meals can easily be adapted. At an Italian restaurant, for instance, you can ask for egg-free pasta or pizza and tell them to omit the cheese. If they're not too familiar with veganism, tell them that you need a vegetarian option that is also egg- and dairy-free. I usually ask for pasta with sautéed vegetables, fresh herbs, and a little olive oil. At Asian restaurants, you can ask them to replace the meat with tofu or more vegetables; most dishes are cooked in vegetable oil and often have plant-based broths like coconut milk. Even sushi is easy to veganize. Simply ask for vegetable or tofu rolls instead of fish. You can also call or email restaurants ahead of time and ask them to provide a vegan option for you. I've had some of the best meals at restaurants that didn't have a single vegan option on the menu. Don't ever be afraid to make your voice heard and don't think that you're being difficult. Restaurants respond to what their customers want, but they can't know that there is a demand for more vegan options if no one tells them. I've learned that if you are polite and explain your choices, they're often curious and even appreciative. This is especially important if you live in an area without vegan options. I know many people who got their local cafés or restaurants to offer at least one vegan dish after talking to the owners or chef.

At coffee shops, it is now very common to be able to choose from a variety of plant-based milks like soy, coconut, and almond, but some coffee shops in rural areas still only serve dairy. If you go there frequently and repeatedly ask for a vegan alternative, they'll be very likely to start serving one soon. Restaurants and cafés care about service first and foremost. They want to make their customers happy while also making a profit, so if there's enough of a demand, they will start providing these options.

People often tell me that one of their main concerns about eating vegan is not knowing how to deal with non-vegan friends inviting them over for lunch and dinner. They don't want to be perceived as rude or difficult by imposing their culinary choices on their hosts. People are sensitive about eating animals and we fear that we'll be judged for our choices. If the tables were turned, however, and you were the host, would you judge someone because they didn't eat certain foods? It is more likely you'd want your guests to feel at ease and comfortable. If someone invites me and they don't know I'm vegan, I thank them for the invitation and say that I'd love to go, but I just want to let them know that I don't eat any animal products. I then offer to bring my own dish in order not to inconvenience them and tell them that they don't have to worry about me or prepare something for me at all. In 90 percent of cases, they tell me that it's not a problem and that they'll gladly provide a vegan option, which I have learned to just accept and show my appreciation for. If they feel uncomfortable because they don't know how to cook vegan dishes or don't want to have to cook two separate meals, I'm more than happy to bring my own dish and have them try it.

BEING VEGAN IN A NON-VEGAN WORLD

While the percentage of vegans worldwide is rapidly growing, most people still do consume animal products, and dealing with that is by far the most unexpectedly challenging aspect of going vegan. When I became a vegan, I was very surprised and overwhelmed by how many people seemed to have a problem with my decision. I loved telling others about my newfound love for veganism, but instead of being met with encouragement or curiosity, I often encountered defensive and almost hostile responses. Light conversations frequently became heated debates, leaving me feeling confused and emotionally drained.

Removing NON-VEGAN ITEMS FROM YOUR KITCHEN

If you decide to go vegan long-term, you will no longer need many of the items in your kitchen. There are two ways to remove everything that is not vegan from your kitchen: You can either do it all at once or you can do it gradually. Which option you choose really depends on your personality, preferred approach, and financial situation. I recommend doing it all at once, as it will help motivate you and reduce the risk of feeling tempted by non-vegan foods. If you don't want to waste food, you can give the products you no longer wish to keep to your neighbors or friends, or donate them. For some people this may not be an option for financial reasons, so if you prefer or need to transition gradually, that is absolutely okay. Simply use up the products you still have while making sure that everything you buy thereafter is vegan.

In an attempt to share the truth about factory farming, I had made it my mission to tell people what I wish I had known years sooner, not realizing that I came across as a little too insistent or even condescending. After months of senselessly arguing with those around me, I felt tired and increasingly drained. I finally made the decision to stop insisting as much. Instead, I asked my friends and family how they genuinely felt, while consciously trying not to make them feel pressured or judged. There is a big difference between what you say and what people hear or interpret. When I said things like "I am vegan because I care about animals," other people would hear, "You're not vegan, so you don't care about animals." The most important thing I've learned when it comes to those situations is to take a step back and try to see things from the other person's perspective. We eat meat because the society we live in makes us believe that it is normal and there is nothing wrong with it. Change requires slowly reconnecting the dots and unlearning so much of what you've been taught all your life. I have learned not to expect immediate results and not to get frustrated when people seemed uninterested. Instead, think of it like planting seeds. Even if someone doesn't show an immediate reaction, you never know how your words will affect them in the long run. I've had people laugh at me for being vegan and then call me three years later to tell me they were now vegan themselves. If they're not ready, the more you insist, the less open to it they'll be. That doesn't mean that you shouldn't talk about veganism at all. Veganism is not a trend or something you should keep to yourself in order not to annoy people— it's an ethical stance that seeks to end the suffering of animals, so spreading this message is very important, but it's just as important to be diplomatic in the way you approach the conversation.

The UNDERCOVER APPROACH

Here's a tip for those who don't want to have to deal with people's reactions when transitioning to a vegan lifestyle. A close friend of mine decided to go vegan a few years ago, but the thought of his friends and family, who all loved meat and cheese, watching his every step and pressuring him was intimidating. So he went vegan but chose not to tell anyone. Much to his surprise, no one noticed. For months, he'd just choose vegan options, without using the word "vegan." Whenever someone did notice that he was eating differently, he simply said that he didn't feel like eating meat or cheese that day. He did this for several months, until he felt comfortable enough to tell the people in his life. Doing this may not be the best solution for everyone, but it took the pressure off him and allowed him to adapt to his new lifestyle without having to deal with people's immediate reactions.

At the end of the day, this is your journey. You'll inevitably encounter some unexpected reactions or unwanted comments, but try not to let them get to you. In the same way, the way in which you choose to spread this message is up to you. All I can tell you is that it helps to remember what it used to be like and to meet people exactly where they are.

Part

FOUR

Beyond the Reset:

Additional Recipes

THE IMPORTANCE OF WATER

The best way to ensure that you stay hydrated throughout the day is to eat fresh fruits and vegetables and to drink plenty of water. How much water you need to drink can vary depending on how hydrating the food you eat is, how active you are, and what kind of climate you live in.

The human brain is made up of about 75 percent water and the average adult human body of 50 to 65 percent water. Water is essential for our survival and optimum health. Here are some of its functions in the human body:

- Forms saliva (which is needed for digestion)
- Allows the body's cells to grow, reproduce, and survive
- Allows the brain to manufacture hormones and neurotransmitters
- Regulates body temperature (through sweating and respiration)
- Helps deliver oxygen throughout the body
- Flushes body waste

Are You Dehydrated?

Staying hydrated is incredibly important, but dehydration has become so common that we often either don't recognize or ignore the signs. Some of the symptoms of dehydration include:

- Increased thirst (thirst is a sign that you are already dehydrated, so try to make sure you drink enough water as a general rule, not only when you're thirsty)
- Feeling overly tired and sleepy (especially when you know you're getting enough sleep)
- Decreased urine output, and/or dark urine (it should be clear like water; the darker your urine, the more dehydrated you are)
- Headaches
- Dizziness
- Dry skin
- Dry eyes (which you'll notice even more if you're wearing contact lenses)
- Eye twitching

Here are some of the best ways to make sure you stay hydrated:

- Start and end your days with water and/or herbal tea

- Eat plenty of fresh fruits and vegetables, as they're very high in water content. The more fresh produce you consume, the less extra water you'll need to drink.

- Drink at least six to eight glasses of water throughout the day (needs can vary, so pay attention to your own body's signs)

- Drink more when you're exercising

- Drink more in warmer climates

Bottled Water

Plastic bottles are detrimental to the environment (watch the documentary *Tapped* for a closer look into this industry and its consequences). If you have no other choice than to drink bottled water, use your own glass bottles and/or other recyclable and BPA-free containers.

How to Move Away from Soda

Many people are or were at some point practically addicted to soda and other sugary drinks. I myself used to drink liters of diet cola a day while practically not drinking water at all. I was so hooked on soda that plain water seemed boring to me. Soda is essentially caffeinated water with added sugar and artificial flavorings. It's one of the number-one things to avoid when your goal is to adopt healthier eating habits and/or to lose weight. If you're having a hard time removing soda from your diet or replacing it with water, try to create your own, healthy soda at home. A great way to transition away from soda is to add lemon juice and ice cubes to sparkling water, or even mix in a little freshly squeezed orange juice to make it sweeter. It may take a little getting used to, but you'll be surprised to see just how quickly your taste buds can adapt. The following recipes for vitamin-infused waters and hot infusions are some other great alternatives.

VITAMIN-
Infused
WATER

Slice or chop fruit, add it to an empty glass jar (16 to 32 ounces), add fresh herbs, and then fill the jar with water and store it in the fridge overnight. Drink it the next day.

SUGGESTED COMBINATIONS

Peach, kiwi, and rosemary

Cherry, lime, and basil

Citrus: grapefruit, orange, lemon, lime

Blueberry, raspberry, strawberry, and mint

Strawberry and lime

Cucumber and lemon

Blueberry and mint

Peach and basil

Grapefruit and rosemary

Raspberry, kiwi, and cilantro

Orange and basil

Cucumber and peach

Note: The amount of fruit you use depends on your desired flavor intensity. Even a little fruit will do. One sliced lemon is more than enough for a 32-ounce jar of water. Also note that some fruits, like grapefruits, can have a very overpowering taste, so use only very little of those. Make sure you wash your fruit thoroughly before adding it to the jar. In the case of citrus fruit, you can also simply squeeze the juice into the jar instead of using the whole fruit.

When using fruits such as cherries or strawberries, you'll want to slice them prior to adding to the water to extract more flavor. In order to reduce overall waste, you can refill your infused water container a few times throughout the day without changing the fruit. You can even blend the fruit into a smoothie at the end of the day to eliminate all waste.

INFUSIONS

When it's gloomy out or you find yourself a bit under the weather, a hot infused drink could be exactly what you're looking for! I've listed some of my favorite hot infusions here, as well as some coffee-based drinks. Many drinks you'll find at coffee shops contain unnecessary additives that aren't always vegan and certainly are not the healthiest, so making your own is a great alternative.

To make the Ginger-Lemon Infusion, Sweet Mint Infusion, Sweet Lemon or Lime Infusion, and Apple Cider Elixir. Place all ingredients in a mug or cup, then let sit for a few minutes before enjoying.

Note: Each of the following recipes makes 1 serving. The amount of each ingredient depends on the amount of water you wish to infuse and how strong you'd like the flavor to be. Also, be sure to use hot but not boiling water.

Ginger-Lemon Infusion

½-inch piece fresh ginger, sliced
Juice of ½ lemon
1 to 2 cups hot water

Sweet Mint Infusion

Handful of fresh mint leaves
2 teaspoons maple syrup
1 to 2 cups hot water

Sweet Lemon or Lime Infusion

1 lemon or lime, sliced
2 teaspoons to 1 tablespoon coconut nectar
1 to 2 cups hot water

Apple Cider Elixir

1 tablespoon apple cider vinegar
Juice of 1 lime
1 tablespoon maple syrup
1 to 2 cups hot water

Sweet Lemon Infusion

SWEET MINT INFUSION

SWEET LIME INFUSION

HOT
DRINKS

To make the Turmeric Golden Milk and Hot Chocolate: Heat the milk in a pot until hot but not boiling. Blend all of the ingredients in a blender or with an immersion blender and enjoy!

Turmeric Golden Milk

1½ cups almond milk

1 to 2 teaspoons maple syrup

1 teaspoon coconut oil

¼-inch piece fresh turmeric, grated (or ½ teaspoon ground turmeric)

½ teaspoon grated fresh ginger

⅛ teaspoon vanilla bean paste

Pinch of ground cardamom

Pinch of ground cinnamon

Hot Chocolate

1½ cups coconut milk

1 to 2 teaspoons maple syrup (or 2 pitted Medjool dates)

1 tablespoon cacao powder

1 teaspoon coconut butter

½ teaspoon maca powder

½ pinch chili powder (optional)

⅛ teaspoon vanilla extract

Pinch of sea salt

Pinch of ground cinnamon

Note: Blending hot liquids can cause pressure buildup inside the blender, causing the lid to burst off and risking burns. As safety precautions, do not fill the blender more than halfway full with hot liquids, and remove the center cap from the lid and cover it with a towel instead, to vent the steam. Alternatively, you can use an immersion blender, or blend all the room-temperature ingredients first and then heat the mixture in a pot.

HOT
CHOCOLATE

TURMERIC
GOLDEN MILK

PUMPKIN SPICE
LATTE
(PAGE 164)

COFFEE-BASED
DRINKS

Each of the following recipes makes 1 serving

Hot Vanilla Latte

1 cup cashew milk
½ cup freshly brewed coffee
1 to 2 pitted Medjool dates
1 teaspoon coconut butter
¼ teaspoon vanilla bean paste

1. Blend all of the ingredients together in a blender or with an immersion blender, then enjoy!

Note: You can turn this into a caramel latte by adding 2 to 3 teaspoons homemade Tahini Caramel Sauce (page 272).

Pumpkin Spice Latte

1 cup cashew milk
½ cup freshly brewed coffee
2 teaspoons maple syrup
½ teaspoon pumpkin pie spice

1. Blend all of the ingredients together in a blender or with an immersion blender, then enjoy!

Maple-Pecan Latte

Latte
⅓ cup pecans, soaked in water (see page 29)
1 cup water
Pinch of sea salt
2 teaspoons maple syrup
1 double shot (2 ounces) espresso or freshly brewed coffee

Toppings
½ teaspoon maple syrup (optional)
⅛ teaspoon vanilla extract (optional)
½ pecan, very finely chopped

1. Blend the soaked pecans, the water, and the salt in a blender until smooth.

2. Filter the pecan milk into a small pot through a nut milk bag and stir in the maple syrup.

3. Heat the maple-pecan milk until very hot but not boiling. Use a milk frother to make it foamy.

4. Pour the espresso into a cup and add the maple-pecan milk. Top with the foam.

5. For the toppings, mix the maple syrup with the vanilla extract, if using, and drizzle on top, then add the chopped pecan.

Note: You can turn any of these recipes into iced drinks by not heating the milk, and adding a cup of ice cubes to your jar, cup, mug, or glass.

MAPLE-PECAN LATTE

JUICES

Why (or why not) juice?

By removing the fiber, you essentially also skip digesting the food. Our bodies prioritize digestion over detoxification, so the less work you make your digestive system do, the more your body can detoxify and rest. Juicing also allows you to consume a very concentrated amount of nutrients in a very short time, more than you would by eating whole fruits and vegetables by themselves, simply because you wouldn't be able to consume the high quantity of produce it takes to make juice. That being said, fruits and vegetables contain fiber for a reason. It's essential for proper digestion and ensures that fructose enters the blood stream slowly. That is why juicing is great as an addition to a whole foods plant-based diet or during a temporary cleanse, but it shouldn't replace whole foods all of the time.

Which juicer should you use?

For most citrus juice, a simple citrus press will do, but to make any other juice, you'll need a juicer. There are different types: centrifuges and slow juicers. (Juice bars or juice companies often use a bigger machine, referred to as an industrial cold press.) A centrifuge system uses a high-speed motor to quickly extract the juice. Because it is so fast, the motor generates heat (which technically speaking means that the juice is no longer raw). The heat causes oxidization and so the juice loses some of its nutrients. Centrifuge juicers that are on the cheaper end also tend to extract a little less juice overall. Slow juicers, on the other hand, use a masticating system, pressing the juice out of the fruits and vegetables by crushing them. They extract more juice and are generally considered better, but they're also more expensive. They also take longer and, with some models, the juice will need to be strained (with a strainer or nut milk bag) if you want it to be completely fiber-free.

Before buying a juicer, here are a few questions you may want to ask yourself so that you can make the most informed decision:

Do you really need a juicer? When is it worth investing in a juicer?

How often will you be using the juicer? If you are planning a juice cleanse or you want to incorporate juices into your daily routine or drink it a few times a week, then I'd say it's definitely worth it. Most high-quality juices at juice bars cost around $8 to $12 for a 16-ounce drink, which may be okay as an occasional treat, but quickly becomes expensive if you buy them regularly.

I wanted to know how much exactly I would save if I made my own juices and if it would justify investing in a pricier juicer. Buying produce in bulk and prioritizing local and seasonal fruits and vegetables, I was able to make my own juice for about $3 to $5 per 16-ounce serving, a savings of about 50 to 70 percent compared to buying at a juice bar. But if you only want to make juice very occasionally, it might be smarter to skip the juicer and get your occasional juice at a juice bar.

WATERMELON COOLER
(PAGE 172)

What is your budget?

A household juicer can cost anywhere from $30 to over $2,000 for a smaller cold press juicer. The most common (good) centrifuges cost $70 to $150 and up. Slow juicers usually cost $200 to $500, although you can find some for $100. If you believe that a juicer will help you and you want to invest in a higher-quality slow juicer, it might be worth saving up or looking into payment plans (some department stores have them, for instance). But if that is not an option for you, then a centrifuge will still be better than no juicer.

What is important to you? (Quality? Time? Easy to use and clean?)

Price is not the only reason a centrifuge might actually be better for you. A centrifuge is faster than a slow juicer, so if you're extremely busy, this might make more sense for you. An expensive juicer won't serve you at all if it remains unused. Another important aspect to consider is how easy to clean the juicer is. All companies will claim that their juicers are both easy to use and easy to clean. The best way to find out if that is true is to read customer reviews online. Also take into consideration how much space the juicer takes up; look for the dimensions in the product description.

Can you juice without a juicer?

Yes. You can blend fruits and vegetables and then strain them using a nut milk bag (this will not work using a strainer), but this will take a lot of time and I'd only recommend this as an occasional or temporary solution, not for regular juicing (unless you don't mind the process). One juice that can easily be made this way is watermelon juice (you could actually also use a strainer for this instead of a nut milk bag, since watermelons don't contain as much fiber). Add some fresh mint leaves and ice cubes to the glass or jar after straining to make it even more refreshing.

What can you juice?

Only certain fruits and vegetables are suited for juicing—ones that taste good *and* yield a lot of juice. For example, bell peppers do taste great when juiced, but they don't yield a lot of juice, so they're not ideal for juicing. The same goes for kiwis, peaches, persimmons, bananas, mangoes, and strawberries (all of those are great in smoothies, though).

- **Fruits that are great for juicing include:** apples, pears, citrus (oranges, lemons, limes, grapefruits), grapes, pineapples, and watermelons.

- **Vegetables that are great for juicing include:** carrots, celery, lettuce, fennel, cucumbers, sweet potatoes, beets, kale, and spinach.

- **Roots:** Ginger and turmeric are wonderful enhancers, but just make sure you don't use too much at once, since they have a rather intense taste.

- **Herbs:** Some of the best are basil, parsley, and cilantro. You won't get much juice out of those, but their taste is strong enough to give your juice a little extra boost.

What are good fruit-veggie combinations?

The greener the juice, the better. Generally speaking, I'd say that if you just want to juice fruit, you might be better off eating the fruit, or making smoothies, instead of juicing it. The fiber in the fruit ensures that the fructose enters your system slowly. Without any fiber, you might feel a bit of a sugar rush (although fructose is not comparable to refined sugar; this isn't the same as drinking sugary soda). Orange juice that still has the pulp in it and watermelon juice, which is very high in water, are exceptions. But generally, balancing fruit with greens ensures that your juices aren't too sweet and also adds extra minerals and vitamins. Combining leafy greens and other vegetables with apples for sweetness is one great pairing. If you don't need any sweetness, feel free to juice greens and other vegetables by themselves.

Should you do a juice cleanse? And if yes, for how long?

The short answer is: Yes, but only if you want to. A juice cleanse is a period of time in which you drink juices instead of eating solid-food meals. A juice cleanse is not something you need to do. Your body detoxifies itself; no food can do that in its place. Cleanses and products that claim to be detoxifying can actually help you detoxify, but only because they replace processed foods, allowing your body to get a break and do the actual work. The fewer toxins and hard-to-digest foods it has to deal with, the more time it can spend cleansing and healing itself. This means that you can achieve similar results to those of a juice cleanse by simply removing processed foods and eating a clean diet like the 28-day reset. Juicing will, however, seem more intense since you're additionally removing all the fiber. If you dislike the feeling of not eating at all, don't torture yourself unnecessarily; it's really not everyone's cup of tea and that's okay. Juicing can, however, feel great to some people. I do it more for the mental than the physical benefits: It feels good to not have to think about food for a while and it puts me in a positive frame of mind. Another added bonus is that, after a juice cleanse, I always start craving healthier foods more than desserts or processed foods.

If you decide to try a juice cleanse, five to seven days is ideal, long enough for you to get over the adaptation or detox phase of the first few days, but not so long that it will require tremendous effort and or willpower (although it won't be the easiest thing you'll ever do, either). If you're planning a longer juice fast, please consult a health practitioner beforehand.

Most people drink about 3 quarts of juice a day during a cleanse, either in six smaller portions or in 1-quart portions three times a day, at mealtimes (I prefer the latter). The juice is hydrating enough for you not to need extra water, but feel free to drink as much water as you want or need. It helps curb any hunger feelings you might experience in between juices. You can also drink herbal teas; just try to avoid caffeinated beverages.

Note: If you'd like to find out more about juicing, I highly recommend the documentary *Fat, Sick & Nearly Dead* (and its sequel, *Fat, Sick & Nearly Dead II*) by Joe Cross. Joe decided to do a juice cleanse for health reasons and combined his experience with a road trip throughout the United States. A truly inspiring documentary.

Should you exercise during a juice cleanse?

Technically, you could, since you're still consuming calories and will therefore have the energy to do so. But the more you rest during the cleanse, the greater the benefits. If you're feeling overly tired, it's better to allow yourself to sleep an extra couple of hours than to exercise. Remember that cleanses like these should only be short-term, so you won't miss out by not exercising for a few days. If you want to keep moving, going for a walk or doing a restorative exercise like yoga or tai chi is ideal. Do not do a juice cleanse just to lose weight quickly and especially do not add a rigorous workout routine thinking you'll lose weight faster. A "quick fix" rarely works because people go right back to their old eating and lifestyle habits. Think of a juice cleanse more like a mini vacation for your body, a kind of reset if you will, so you can slowly but surely incorporate healthier habits into your day-to-day life and ensure long-term results.

Incorporating juicing in your day-to-day life

The best way to start including fresh juices on a daily (or weekly) basis is by having a green juice before breakfast. Try to enjoy juices before heavier meals rather than after. They digest much more quickly and it'll therefore be better for your digestive system. If you want to have a juice to replace a meal, you can do that too, but you'll need to make sure it's big enough that you get sufficient calories. A 32-ounce juice has about 400 calories (the exact amount varies depending on the fruit-veggie ratio).

"*Perhaps in the back of our minds we already understand, without all the science I've discussed, that something terribly wrong is happening. Our sustenance now comes from misery. We know that if someone offers to show us a film on how our meat is produced, it will be a horror film. We perhaps know more than we care to admit, keeping it down in the dark places of our memory—disavowed. When we eat factory-farmed meat we live, literally, on tortured flesh. Increasingly, that tortured flesh is becoming our own.*"

—Jonathan Safran Foer, *Eating Animals*

FRESH
JUICES

Juicing, once you have your juicer, is relatively easy. Simply cut the fruits and vegetables, peel them when necessary (citrus, for instance, but produce with a thinner skin, like apples, doesn't need to be peeled), and run them through the juicer. Here are some suggested ingredient combinations; all make 1 serving, although the total volume will vary:

Simple Green Love

2 cups kale
2 cups fresh spinach leaves
2 green apples
1 lemon
¼-inch piece fresh ginger

Grapefruit-Fennel Delight

2 celery stalks
1 pear (or apple)
1 grapefruit
¼ fennel bulb

Immune Booster

3 carrots
2 celery stalks
1 apple
½ beet
¼-inch piece fresh turmeric

The Greenest Green

½ head romaine
1 cup kale
1 cucumber
2 celery stalks
1 lemon

Note: This juice is extremely healthy and will not have a sweet taste

Pineapple Delight

3 cups pineapple
4 leaves lacinato kale
Handful of fresh parsley leaves
Handful of fresh mint leaves
1 lemon
¼-inch piece fresh ginger

Turmeric Orange Booster

3 large oranges
½-inch piece fresh turmeric
¼ cucumber

Watermelon Cooler

Makes 2 small or 1 large

½ small watermelon
½ cucumber
1 handful fresh mint
1 lime

PINEAPPLE DELIGHT

GRAPEFRUIT-FENNEL
DELIGHT

SIMPLE GREEN LOVE

TURMERIC ORANGE BOOSTER

THE
GREENEST
GREEN

IMMUNE BOOSTER

Juices vs. Smoothies

Smoothies and juices each have their own advantages. While juices allow you to get a quicker energy kick and nutrients in a more concentrated form, smoothies are more filling thanks to the fiber they contain. They also require less produce to make, so they tend to be a little cheaper. Smoothies make filling meal replacements, because you can also add a little fat and protein.

In order to make a great smoothie, it's important to know which ingredients combine well. A sweet, fruity base is the best place to start, using either frozen fruit or ripe fresh fruit. Some fruits that are great in smoothies are bananas, mangoes, oranges, pineapple, peaches, dates, apples, and berries. Some vegetables that combine well with fruits in smoothies are spinach, kale, butter lettuce, romaine lettuce, cucumber, zucchini, celery, Swiss chard, and arugula. Frozen cauliflower has also become a very popular smoothie ingredient, as it adds a creamy texture without adding too much sweetness. The trick to making a great green smoothie is not to overdo it. If you add too many greens, your smoothie may start tasting like a soup rather than a smoothie. To find the right amount for you, start with a little, taste test, and then add some more if you wish. If you've accidentally added too much, simply blend in a little more fruit.

Add ½ to 1 cup liquid—water, plant-based milk, or fruit juice—per 2 cups fruit and greens. The more liquid you add, the thinner its consistency will be. You can also add some fat and/or protein, in the form of hemp seeds, chia seeds, or ground flaxseed; nut butters or nuts; coconut butter or oil; avocado; or plant-based protein powder (make sure it's clearly vegan and doesn't contain whey or casein). For a 16-ounce smoothie, add between 1 teaspoon and 2 tablespoons seeds or nuts/nut butter, ¼ to ½ of an avocado, and/or 1 scoop protein powder. For an extra kick, you can add grated fresh ginger or turmeric or superfood powders such as maca, chlorella, spirulina, acai, wheatgrass, barley grass juice powder, and beet root powder. Or add flavorings like extracts, ground cinnamon, cacao or carob powder, or fresh herbs like basil and cilantro.

If you're not using frozen fruit, you may want to add a few ice cubes to your smoothie. Room temperature or refrigerated smoothies are perfectly fine, but adding at least one frozen ingredient will make it much more refreshing, especially on a hot day.

If possible, smoothies should be prepared right before you drink them. Luckily, they are quick to make. If you want to prepare a smoothie to drink at work, do so right before leaving home and keep it in a thermos, then store it in a fridge at work if you can until you're ready to drink it.

Note: If you want to have smoothies for breakfast, but prefer eating rather than drinking your food, use a little less liquid and transfer the smoothie to a bowl. Add the toppings of your choice, like dried fruits, quick-cooking oats, nuts, seeds, and/or nut butters, and eat it with a spoon.

Smoothie Cleanse

I mentioned this on page 17, but it bears repeating. Your body detoxifies itself—a specific food or ingredient cannot do that in its place. But eating and drinking unprocessed fruits and vegetables can help support your body's detoxifying functions.

Nutritionally speaking, consuming only smoothies for a certain amount of time isn't necessarily more beneficial than just eating fresh, whole foods, but it does make eating fruits and vegetables a little easier, since you won't have to spend as much time thinking about what to eat or preparing your foods. You can use a short smoothie cleanse (one to seven or even ten days) to jump-start healthier eating habits.

"We patronize them for their incompleteness, for their tragic fate for having taken form so far below ourselves. And therein do we err. For the animal shall not be measured by man. In a world older and more complete than ours, they move finished and complete, gifted with the extension of the senses we have lost or never attained, living by voices we shall never hear. They are not brethren, they are not underlings: they are other nations, caught with ourselves in the net of life and time, fellow prisoners of the splendour and travail of the earth."

—Henry Beston

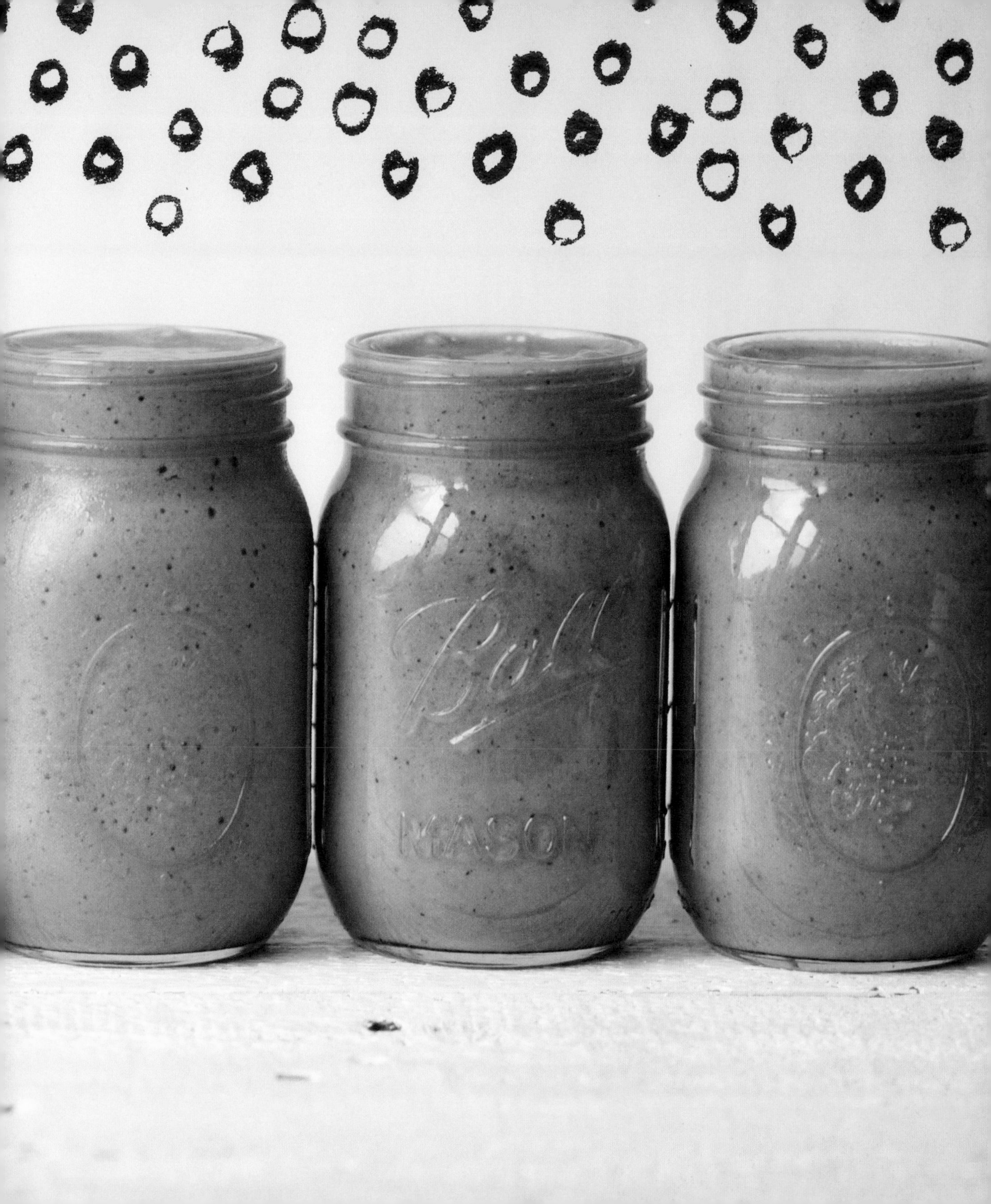
Ball
MASON

SMOOTHIES

Blend all of the ingredients in a blender, pour into a glass or jar, and enjoy! Here are some of my favorite smoothie combinations. Each recipe makes one serving of about 16 ounces.

Blue Medjool Smoothie

2 frozen bananas

1 cup fresh blueberries

½ cup water

2 pitted Medjool dates

2 tablespoons whole almonds

1 teaspoon maca powder

Soul Shine Smoothie

2 bananas

¾ cup frozen peaches

¾ cup frozen mango chunks

½ cup water

5 to 10 basil leaves

½-inch piece fresh ginger, peeled and grated

1 teaspoon hemp seeds

Littlefoot Smoothie

1 banana

2 lacinato kale leaves

½ celery stalk

1 cup frozen mango chunks

½ papaya

½ cup coconut water

2 teaspoons ground flaxseed

Coconut-Lemon Cheesecake Smoothie

2 frozen bananas

¾ cup coconut water

½ cup cashews

Juice of ½ lemon

3 pitted Medjool dates

1 tablespoon unsweetened shredded coconut

½ teaspoon vanilla extract

Cinnanut Smoothie

2 frozen bananas

1 cup mixed baby greens

½ cup almond milk

2 tablespoons cashews

2 tablespoons hazelnuts

1 tablespoon cacao powder

½ teaspoon vanilla extract

½ teaspoon ground cinnamon

Epic Sunshine Smoothie

1 cup frozen mango chunks

1 cup frozen peaches

1 banana

½ cup carrot juice

½ cup coconut water

2 teaspoons ground flaxseed

· CONTINUES ·

Blue Medjool Smoothie

COCONUT-LEMON CHEESECAKE SMOOTHIE

SOUL SHINE SMOOTHIE

"BASIL EVERYTHING" SMOOTHIE

Mango Lime Froyo

Solero Smoothie

2½ cups frozen mango chunks

¼ cup freshly squeezed blood orange juice

¼ cup freshly squeezed orange juice

¼ cup carrot juice

2 teaspoons ground flaxseed

Perfect Post-Workout Green Smoothie

1 cup frozen peach slices

1 cup fresh spinach leaves

½ cup freshly squeezed orange juice

½ mango, peeled and pit removed

⅓ cup ice cubes

½ handful of fresh basil leaves

2 teaspoons hemp seeds

1 teaspoon chia seeds

Petit Gervais Smoothie

1½ cups frozen strawberries

1 cup fresh spinach leaves

½ cup water

1 peach, pitted

½ ripe pear

¼ avocado

3 pitted Medjool dates

Better Than Coffee Smoothie

1 cup frozen pineapple

1 cup curly kale

½ cup freshly squeezed orange juice

½ cup fresh spinach leaves

½ handful fresh basil leaves

1 teaspoon spirulina

Sweet Green Banana Smoothie

2 frozen bananas

1 cup romaine lettuce

½ cup water

¼ cucumber

½ handful of fresh basil leaves

¼-inch piece fresh ginger, peeled and grated

½ teaspoon vanilla extract

Sweet Peanut Butter Cup Smoothie

2 frozen bananas

½ cup almond milk

1 tablespoon cacao powder

1 tablespoon peanut butter

1 teaspoon coconut butter

½ teaspoon vanilla extract

PB&J Smoothie

2 bananas

½ cup frozen raspberries (see Note)

½ cup frozen blueberries (see Note)

½ cup cashew milk

2 tablespoons peanut butter

Note: You may use any kind of frozen berries.

The "Basil Everything" Smoothie

½ ripe mango, peeled and pitted

⅓ cup ice cubes

¼ cup freshly squeezed grapefruit juice

¼ cup freshly squeezed tangerine juice

¼ cup frozen cherries

8 to 10 fresh basil leaves

1 teaspoon ground flaxseed

Chocolate Mousse Smoothie

2 to 3 frozen bananas

½ to ¾ cup coconut milk (use ½ cup if you're using 2 bananas; ¾ cup for 3)

2 tablespoons cacao powder

1 tablespoon coconut butter

Mango Lime Froyo

Smoothie

2 cups frozen mango chunks

Juice of 1 lime

½ cup plant-based yogurt (like coconut, soy, or almond)

1 teaspoon maple syrup

1 tablespoon ground flaxseed

Toppings

2 strawberries, sliced

1 tablespoon unsweetened shredded coconut

1. Blend all the smoothie ingredients until smooth, adding a little more yogurt if necessary until it reaches the desired consistency. Top with the toppings and enjoy!

SWEET PEANUT BUTTER CUP
SMOOTHIE

CHOCOLATE MOUSSE
SMOOTHIE

PB&J
SMOOTHIE

VEGAN MILKS (OR MYLK)

Most of us grew up in households where milk was part of day-to-day life. However, as humans, we have no biological need for the milk of other non-human animals. It is normal, then, to seek an alternative to dairy milk. Luckily, there are so many different plant-based milks available that you can easily find one you like and that suits you best. Keep in mind that the taste will never match that of cow's milk entirely, but remember that your taste buds will adapt to new flavors in about ten to fifteen days, so if you don't immediately like the taste of vegan milk, try a different kind or give it a few more chances.

While you can find plant-based milks almost anywhere now, there are three good reasons to make your own instead. At the end of the day, do what works best for you. I personally switch between buying store-bought milk and making my own when I feel like it.

- **Cost:** Some brands are more affordable than others, but if the only brands available to you are too expensive, making your own is a great alternative.

- **Less processed:** In order to increase a product's shelf life, it has to be processed, even if just minimally. Nondairy milks you make at home are less processed than those you buy at the store.

- **More eco-friendly:** When making your own milk, you avoid the packaging that comes with store-bought versions, eliminating waste.

COCONUT MILK   CASHEW MILK   ALMOND MILK   SOY MILK

NUT MILKS

MAKES 3½ TO 4 CUPS

Probably one of the most popular options as a base for plant-based milks are nuts and seeds. They're extremely versatile and can easily be turned into a variety of dairy alternatives, like milk, yogurt, ice cream, or even cheese. What you'll need:

Nuts: Almonds, cashews, Brazil nuts, hazelnuts, walnuts . . . you can use any nut you like or a combination of two or more different ones (to make walnut-almond milk, for instance).

Blender: High-speed blenders are ideal, but any blender will do, as you'll soak the nuts beforehand.

Nut milk bag: If you want creamy, smooth milk, you'll have to strain it. A nut milk bag (you can find inexpensive ones in health food stores or online) is ideal, but a very fine-mesh strainer will do, too.

Note: Some people choose to leave the pulp in the milk, which will make it a lot more nutritious but not as enjoyable to drink. If you do strain it, you can keep and freeze the pulp for later use. It's a great base for healthy vegan desserts and breakfast bowls.

Nut Milk
1 cup raw nuts, soaked in water for about 12 hours and then drained
3½ cups filtered water (room temperature or hot, but not boiling)
Pinch of sea salt

Optional Sweeteners
2 to 4 pitted Medjool dates, soaked in water and then drained
1 tablespoon maple syrup, brown rice syrup, or stevia (depending on how sweet you like it; if you use the nut milk in smoothies, you don't need to sweeten it at all)

Optional Flavorings
Vanilla bean seeds
Cacao powder
Ground cinnamon
Ground turmeric
Strawberries
Banana

1. Blend the nuts with the water and salt in a blender for at least 1 minute, until smooth. Refrigerate the milk until cool, which will make it creamier.

2. Strain the milk into a container using a nut milk bag or a very fine strainer.

3. Blend the strained milk with any of the optional sweeteners or flavorings.

4. Pour the milk into a container and close it with a lid. Refrigerate for up to 3 or 4 days (in the coolest spot possible, which is usually in the back, away from the door). Shake your milk well before drinking it!

STRAWBERRY NUT MILK   CACAO NUT MILK   BANANA NUT MILK

More
NONDAIRY
MILKS

Seed Milks

You can use a variety of seeds like chia, hemp, or sesame seeds to make deliciously creamy seed milks. Blend about 1 cup seeds with 2 cups water (depending on desired creaminess and consistency), then blend in any sweeteners or flavorings of choice. Tip: You can also use tahini to make sesame milk, which will be a lot quicker than starting with whole sesame seeds!

Oat Milk

Mix 1 cup oats with 4 cups hot, but not boiling, water and place in a mason jar in the fridge overnight. In the morning, blend and strain the mixture, add sweeteners and flavorings of choice, and blend again. Enjoy!

Rice Milk

Makes 4 cups

1 cup cooked rice

4 cups water

Pinch of sea salt

½ teaspoon vanilla extract (optional)

Sweetener or flavoring of choice (see page 184; optional)

1. Blend all the ingredients in a blender until smooth.

2. Strain into a container using a nut milk bag. Keep in the fridge for 3 to 4 days and shake well before drinking.

Note: Rice milk is a great alternative to nut milk if you have nut allergies or you want a version that's a little lower in fat.

Soy Milk

Makes 7 to 8 cups

1 cup organic soybeans
7 to 8 cups water, plus more for
soaking the beans
Sweetener or flavoring of choice
(see page 184; optional)

1. Soak the beans in water
overnight.

2. Drain the beans using a strainer
and remove the skins.

3. Blend the beans with 7 to 8 cups
of the water until smooth.

4. Strain the milk into a pot using
a nut milk bag. Bring to a boil. As
soon as it starts boiling, reduce the
heat to medium-low and cook for
about 20 minutes. Be sure to keep
an eye on it so it doesn't overflow.

5. Let the milk cool to room
temperature, then strain again
using a strainer and blend
with any desired sweeteners or
flavorings, if using. Store in a glass
container with a lid in the fridge
for up to 4 to 5 days. Shake well
before drinking.

Coconut Milk

Simply blend the "flesh" and
water/milk of a mature coconut
and enjoy (no need to strain!).

FRUIT-BASED
ICE CREAM

Homemade vegan ice cream is much easier to make than you might think and it's also much healthier than dairy ice cream. Fruit-based ice creams and sorbets are the quickest, easiest, and healthiest options, so that's what I'm including here, but note that you can also make your own coconut milk– or soy milk–based ice cream using an ice cream machine.

Banana Ice Cream

Start with frozen bananas for the base (see page 26 for how to freeze bananas). If you use a food processor, simply break the frozen bananas into smaller chunks and add them to the food processor one by one, processing until you get an ice cream–like consistency. In a high-speed blender, add all the frozen banana pieces at once and blend them into ice cream, using the blender's stopper to move the bananas around. Important: Only use a stopper if it's part of your blender. If yours doesn't have one, turn the blender off and use a spoon or spatula to stir the bananas, remove it, and put the lid back on before turning the blender on again.

If you use an immersion blender or a regular (not high-speed) blender, you'll need to add a little liquid, either water or plant-based milk, and add the banana chunks one by one. If you want your ice cream to be firmer, simply put it in the freezer until fully frozen.

Suggested "Add-Ins"

Sweeteners: Bananas are already very sweet, so you won't need to add any sweeteners, but if you want to, you can add pitted Medjool dates or date syrup.

Flavorings: Feel free to add any flavorings of your choice, such as cacao powder, vanilla extract, mint essence, etc.

Fruits: Other frozen fruits that are a great addition to banana ice cream are blueberries, raspberries, cherries, strawberries, peaches, and mangoes.

· CONTINUES ·

MANGO, PEACH & BASIL SORBET

CHERRY-BANANA ICE CREAM

CHOCOLATE-MINT ICE CREAM

Cherry-Banana Ice Cream

Makes 1 large or 2 small servings

3 frozen bananas
1 cup cherries, pitted, plus more for serving
½ teaspoon vanilla extract
2 tablespoons almonds

1. Blend the bananas, cherries, and vanilla together in a food processor or blender until the mixture reaches a smooth consistency.

2. Top with the additional cherries and the almonds and enjoy!

Note: If you'd like your sorbet to be extra firm, freeze it for 30 to 60 minutes after it's been blended.

Chocolate-Mint Ice Cream

Makes 1 large or 2 small servings

Ice Cream
3 frozen bananas
2 tablespoons cacao powder
¼ to ½ teaspoon peppermint extract

Chocolate Sauce
1 tablespoon maple syrup
1 teaspoon cacao powder
1 teaspoon melted coconut oil
Pinch of sea salt

Toppings
2 tablespoons cacao nibs (or vegan chocolate or carob chips)
½ handful of fresh mint leaves

1. Blend all of the ice cream ingredients in a food processor or blender until smooth.

2. Mix all of the chocolate sauce ingredients together using a fork or whisk, and drizzle over the ice cream.

3. Top with the cacao nibs and mint and enjoy!

Sorbet

Simply blend any juicy frozen fruit of your choice. To make it extra firm, place it in the freezer for an additional 30 to 60 minutes.

Mango, Peach & Basil Sorbet

Makes 1 serving

1 cup frozen mango chunks
1 cup frozen peach slices
¼ cup carrot juice, or coconut water (optional)
Handful of fresh basil leaves, plus a few extra leaves for garnish

1. Blend all of the ingredients in a food processor or blender until smooth.

2. Garnish with basil leaves and enjoy!

Cherry-Mango Pops

Makes 2 servings or several smaller pops, depending on the size of the molds

1 cup pitted cherries
1 large mango, peeled and pitted
1 peach, pitted
⅓ cup orange juice

1. Blend all of the ingredients in a food processor or blender until smooth. Pour into ice pop molds. Freeze for at least a couple of hours, until solid.

Juice Pops & ICE CUBES

You can turn any of the recipes from the section on juicing (see pages 166 to 172) into juice pops by freezing them in ice pop molds or an ice cube tray. Another fun way to refresh your water in the summer is to place single berries and/or herbs in ice cube trays, then fill them with coconut water, lemon-infused water, or plain water. Freeze them overnight and serve them in ice water.

MYLKSHAKES

You can make delicious vegan milkshakes by simply blending any of the ice cream or sorbet bases with an extra ½ to 1 cup of plant-based milk. If you want a version that's a little less sweet or not as fruity, you can add ice cubes instead of frozen fruit. You can also freeze plant-based milk in ice cube trays and then blend the cubes with the ice cream or sorbet base. Here are a few shake ideas:

Blueberry-Vanilla Shake

2 bananas (or 1½ pears, cored and chopped)
1 cup frozen blueberries (preferably wild)
¾ cup almond milk
½ teaspoon vanilla extract

1. Blend all of the ingredients until smooth and enjoy!

Sweet Vanilla Shake

1½ cups ice cubes
1 cup soy milk
4 pitted Medjool dates
1 teaspoon vanilla extract

1. Blend all of the ingredients until smooth and enjoy!

Note: As an alternative, omit the ice cubes and use 2 frozen bananas instead of the dates.

Coco-Cocoa Shake

1 cup coconut milk
1 cup ice cubes
2 frozen bananas
2 tablespoons cacao powder
1 tablespoon coconut butter
¼ teaspoon vanilla extract
1 tablespoon unsweetened shredded coconut

1. Blend the coconut milk, ice cubes, bananas, cacao powder, coconut butter, and vanilla until smooth.

2. Top with the shredded coconut and enjoy!

Orange Creamsicle Shake

1 cup coconut milk
1 cup ice cubes
½ peeled orange (or ½ cup orange juice)
2 pitted Medjool dates

1. Blend all of the ingredients until smooth and enjoy!

COCO-COCOA SHAKE

SWEET VANILLA SHAKE

ORANGE CREAMSICLE SHAKE

BLUEBERRY-VANILLA SHAKE

NUT & SEED BUTTERS

In order to make your own nut and seed butters, all you need is a food processor and a little patience. The best and highest-quality nut and seed butters contain only one ingredient. You can, however, add any flavorings you wish, or combine different nuts and seeds with each other. To make nut butter, it's ideal to roast the nuts on a baking sheet at 350°F/177°C for approximately 5 to 10 minutes, and also to remove the skins for a smoother consistency. Wait until after they are roasted, then use a kitchen towel to rub off and remove the skins. Then, in a food processor or high-speed blender, process them for 8 to 12 minutes until they reach a smooth nut butter consistency. You will have to watch it closely, as the time may vary depending on the type of nuts or seeds you use. Resist the urge to add water. You can also add flavorings such as vanilla extract, ground cinnamon, sea salt, cacao powder, ground turmeric, or ground flaxseed—the possibilities are endless. Feel free to experiment with your favorite combinations. Here are a few of mine:

Roasted hazelnuts and cacao powder

Roasted almonds, cashews, and sea salt

Brazil nuts and macadamia nuts

Sesame seeds and flaxseed (or use sesame seeds by themselves to make homemade tahini)

Roasted walnuts, pecans, and cinnamon

Sunflower seeds and turmeric

Note: It's best to keep nut butter in the fridge to keep it from going rancid, but if you'd like it to be soft when you use it, remove it from the fridge about an hour ahead of time.

> "I am only one, but I am one. I cannot do everything, but I can do something. And I will not let what I cannot do interfere with what I can do."
> —Edward Everett Hale

Toasted & Salted Almond-Pecan Butter

Makes 1 small (4-ounce) jar

2 cups almonds
1 cup pecans
¼ teaspoon sea salt

1. Preheat the oven to 350°F/177°C. Line a baking sheet with parchment paper.

2. Spread the almonds and pecans on the baking sheet and roast for 7 minutes. While they are still warm, use a kitchen towel to rub off and remove the skins.

3. Place the roasted nuts in a food processor or blender, then process on high speed for 6 minutes. Add the salt and blend for 2 more minutes, or longer, until the consistency is creamy.

4. Let cool, then store in an airtight container in the fridge.

White Chocolate Butter

Makes 1 small (4-ounce) jar

2 cups cashews
1 cup macadamia nuts
1 tablespoon coconut oil
3 tablespoons cacao butter
3 tablespoons maple syrup
1 teaspoon vanilla extract
¼ teaspoon sea salt

1. Preheat the oven to 350°F/177°C. Line a baking sheet with parchment paper.

2. Spread the cashews and macadamia nuts on the baking sheet and roast for 7 minutes.

3. Place the roasted nuts in a food processor or blender, then process on high speed for 3 minutes. Add the coconut oil. Blend for 3 more minutes, then add the cacao butter, maple syrup, vanilla, and salt and blend for 2 more minutes.

4. Let cool, then store in an airtight container in the fridge.

Crunchy Salted Peanut Butter

Makes 1 small (4-ounce) jar

3 cups peanuts
½ teaspoon sea salt

1. Preheat the oven to 350°F/177°C. Line a baking sheet with parchment paper.

2. Spread the peanuts on the baking sheet and roast for 8 minutes.

3. Place 2 cups of the roasted nuts in a food processor or blender, then process on high speed for 8 to 10 minutes. Add the salt and the remaining 1 cup peanuts and pulse for a few seconds, until the peanut butter has a chunky consistency.

4. Let cool, then store in an airtight container in the fridge.

TOPPINGS

The following recipes are great additions to salads, soups, stews, and breakfasts, on their own or in combination with spices and other condiments.

Smoky Mix Base for Veggie "Bacon"

Makes ¼ cup

1 tablespoon olive oil
2 teaspoons liquid smoke
1 teaspoon maple syrup
2 pinches of sea salt
¼ teaspoon smoked paprika

1. Mix all ingredients in a small bowl.

Note: You can use this mix on a variety of different vegetables and nuts. Here are a few suggestions and examples. You can also use the smoky mix with eggplant, zucchini, or sliced almonds.

Shiitake Bacon

Makes ⅓ to ½ cup

4 cups shiitake mushrooms, thinly sliced, stems discarded
Smoky Mix Base (left)

1. Preheat the oven to 350°F/177°C. Line a baking sheet with parchment paper.

2. In a bowl, mix the mushrooms with the smoky mix base. Spread them on the baking sheet and bake for about 25 minutes. Check them after 20 minutes to make sure they don't burn. If you want extra-crispy bacon, increase the baking time to 30 to 35 minutes.

3. Let the shiitake bacon cool and then store in an airtight container in the fridge for 3 to 5 days.

Note: Very important: Make sure the mushrooms, carrot bits, or coconut flakes are well coated, mixing with your hands if necessary. Add a little more oil if needed.

Smoky Carrot Bits

Makes ⅓ to ½ cup

2 carrots, thinly sliced using a mandolin or vegetable peeler
Smoky Mix Base (left)

1. Preheat the oven to 350°F/177°C. Line a baking sheet with parchment paper.

2. Chop the carrot slices into even smaller bits and mix them in a bowl with the smoky mix base. Spread them on the baking sheet and bake for about 30 minutes. Check them after 20 to 25 minutes to make sure they don't burn.

3. Let the carrot bits cool and then store in an airtight container in the fridge for 3 to 5 days.

· CONTINUES ·

SMOKY CARROT BITS

SPICY SUNFLOWER SEEDS

COCONUT BACON

SHIITAKE BACON

CURRIED PUMPKIN SEEDS

Coconut Bacon

Makes 2 cups

2 cups unsweetened coconut flakes (not shredded)
3 tablespoons Smoky Mix Base (page 196)

1. Preheat the oven to 350°F/ 177°C. Line a baking sheet with parchment paper.

2. Mix the coconut flakes in a bowl with the smoky mix base. Spread them on the baking sheet and bake for 8 to 10 minutes. Check them after 5 minutes to make sure they don't burn.

3. Let the coconut bacon cool and then store in an airtight container at room temperature for up to 1 week.

Curried Pumpkin Seeds

Makes ½ cup

½ cup pumpkin seeds
1 teaspoon olive oil
½ teaspoon curry powder
¼ teaspoon sea salt

1. Mix the pumpkin seeds with the oil, curry powder, and salt and toast them in a small pan over high heat for 2 to 3 minutes.

Spicy Sunflower Seeds

Makes ½ cup

½ cup sunflower seeds
1 teaspoon olive oil
¼ teaspoon sea salt
¼ teaspoon smoked paprika
¼ teaspoon crushed red pepper flakes
⅛ teaspoon chili powder
Pinch of ground black pepper
Pinch of cayenne pepper

1. Mix the sunflower seeds with the oil, salt, paprika, red pepper flakes, chili powder, black pepper, and cayenne and toast them in a small pan over high heat for about 3 minutes.

Other
INGREDIENTS
THAT CAN BE USED AS
TOPPINGS

Unsweetened dried cranberries, raisins, or other **dried fruit**

Sun-dried tomatoes

Bread crumbs

Nuts, either whole, chopped, or sliced, toasted if you want (Note: Mix nuts like pine nuts or cashews with a little maple syrup to create a candied topping that tastes amazing in pasta dishes)

Seeds

DRESSINGS

Classic Cheesy Tahini Dressing

Makes about ½ cup

3 tablespoons tahini
2 tablespoons nutritional yeast
Juice of 1 lemon
1 teaspoon hemp seeds
¼ teaspoon sea salt
¼ teaspoon garlic powder
Up to ¼ cup water

1. Blend or mix together the tahini, nutritional yeast, lemon juice, hemp seeds, salt, and garlic powder. The mixture should have a thick and creamy consistency.

2. Add the water little by little until the dressing reaches your desired consistency.

Note: Mixing this dressing with a whisk or fork instead of blending it in a blender will make it a little less smooth because of the hemp seeds. Both variations are delicious, so it's up to you which one you prefer. You can also omit the hemp seeds.

TTT Dressing

Makes about ¾ cup

¼ cup tahini
Juice of 3 tangerines (or substitute lemon juice)
1 to 2 tablespoons water
1 tablespoon ground turmeric
Pinch of sea salt

1. Mix all of the ingredients until smooth using a fork or whisk.

Cilantro, Tahini & Lime Dressing

Makes about 1 cup

¼ cup tahini
¼ cup water
Juice of 3 limes
Handful of fresh cilantro leaves
Pinch of sea salt

1. Blend all of the ingredients until smooth.

Ginger-Miso Dressing

Makes about ¾ cup

¼ cup rice vinegar
3 tablespoons olive oil
3 tablespoons sesame seeds
2 tablespoons white miso paste
2 tablespoons tamari or soy sauce
1-inch piece fresh ginger, peeled and grated
¼ teaspoon garlic powder (or 1 clove, minced)
Pinch of ground black pepper

1. Blend all of the ingredients until smooth.

· CONTINUES ·

EGGPLANT DIP

SWEET CHERRY-ALMOND VINAIGRETTE

YOGURT-MINT DRESSING

SWEET AND SMOKY TOMATO SAUCE

TTT DRESSING

SWEET LEMON VINAIGRETTE

BEET & WHITE BEAN DIP

CREAMY BASIL DRESSING

BASIC HUMMUS

SPICY CASHEW DRESSING

CLASSIC CHEESY TAHINI DRESSING

YOGURT-CUCUMBER-DILL DRESSING

VEGAN "HONEY" MUSTARD

GINGER-MISO DRESSING

SPICY PEANUT BUTTER DRESSING

SUNFLOWER-CHIVE CREAM CHEESE DIP

SMOKED PAPRIKA-AVOCADO DIP

CILANTRO, TAHINI & LIME DRESSING

Vegan "Honey" Mustard

Makes ¾ cup

½ cup yellow or Dijon mustard
¼ cup maple syrup, coconut
   nectar, or brown rice syrup

1. Mix the mustard and syrup
using a whisk or a fork.

Note: One serving is about 3 tablespoons, so you can either scale down
the quantities and make this dressing in
smaller quantities whenever you need
it, or make the full batch and store it in
the fridge.

Sweet Lemon Vinaigrette

Makes about ½ cup

3 tablespoons olive oil
3 tablespoons hemp seeds
2 tablespoons apple cider vinegar
2 tablespoons maple syrup
Zest of ½ lemon and juice of the
   whole lemon
Pinch of sea salt

1. Blend all of the ingredients until
smooth.

Note: This will separate while stored,
so make sure to stir with a fork before
using.

Sweet Cherry-Almond Vinaigrette

Makes about 1 cup

⅓ cup fresh cherries, pitted
   (see Note)
⅓ cup olive oil
¼ cup balsamic vinegar
¼ cup sliced blanched almonds
2 tablespoons brown rice syrup
¼ teaspoon sea salt

1. Blend all of the ingredients until
smooth in a food processor or
blender. Use as soon as possible;
you can store it in an airtight
container in the fridge for up to
3 to 5 days. Best when served fresh!

Note: You can substitute frozen
cherries. Cook them in a small pot for
1 to 2 minutes to thaw them before
blending.

Creamy Basil Dressing

Makes ¼ cup

2 cups fresh basil leaves
⅓ cup pine nuts
2 tablespoons olive oil
1 garlic clove, minced
½ teaspoon sea salt

1. Pulse all of the ingredients in a food processor until the dressing reaches a moderately chunky consistency.

Yogurt-Mint Dressing

Makes ¾ cup

½ cup unsweetened coconut yogurt
½ handful of fresh mint leaves
1 garlic clove, minced
Juice of 1 lemon
1 tablespoon apple cider vinegar
Pinch of sea salt

1. Blend all of the ingredients in a blender until smooth.

Note: Instead of blending, you can finely chop the mint leaves and mix the dressing using a fork.

Yogurt-Cucumber-Dill Dressing

Makes ¾ cup

½ cup soy or almond yogurt
½ handful of fresh dill, chopped
⅛ cucumber, very finely chopped
Juice of 1 lemon
1 tablespoon apple cider vinegar
½ teaspoon onion powder
½ teaspoon garlic powder
¼ teaspoon sea salt

1. Mix all of the ingredients using a whisk or a fork.

Note: You could also blend the dressing in a blender. But add the chopped cucumber at the end instead of blending it so that the dressing retains its texture.

Spicy Cashew Dressing

Makes ¾ cup

½ cup cashews, soaked in water (see page 29)
⅓ cup water
Juice of 1 lemon
1 garlic clove, minced (or ¼ teaspoon garlic powder)
½ teaspoon onion powder (or 1 green onion, chopped)
¼ to ½ teaspoon crushed red pepper flakes (optional), to taste
¼ teaspoon smoked paprika
Pinch of cayenne pepper
Pinch of ground black pepper

1. Blend all of the ingredients in a blender until smooth.

Spicy Peanut Butter Dressing

Makes ¾ cup

¼ cup creamy peanut butter
3 tablespoons water
2 tablespoons tamari or soy sauce
Juice of 1 lime
2 teaspoons coconut nectar
¼ teaspoon crushed red pepper flakes
¼ teaspoon garlic powder

1. Mix or blend all of the ingredients until smooth.

DIPS & SAUCES

Eggplant Dip

Makes ½ to ¾ cup

1 eggplant, halved
¼ cup water
3 tablespoons tahini
Juice of 1 lemon
1 garlic clove, minced
Pinch of sea salt
Pinch of ground black pepper
Pinch of cumin

1. Preheat the oven to 400°F/200°C. Line a baking sheet with parchment paper.

2. Set the eggplant on the baking sheet and bake for 60 minutes. When cool enough to handle, remove the skin from the eggplant, then strain to remove all excess liquid.

3. Blend (or mash using a fork) the eggplant with all of the remaining ingredients until smooth.

Basic Hummus

Makes ¾ to 1 cup

1 cup cooked chickpeas (see page 29)
⅓ cup warm water
2 tablespoons olive oil
1 tablespoon tahini
Juice of 1 lemon
1 garlic clove, minced
½ teaspoon sea salt

1. Blend all of the ingredients in a blender or food processor until smooth.

Roasted Bell Pepper Hummus

Makes ¾ to 1 cup

½ red bell pepper
1 teaspoon olive oil
1 batch Basic Hummus
Pinch of sea salt
Up to 2 tablespoons water

1. Cook the bell pepper in the oil in a pan over high heat for 2 to 3 minutes.

2. Let the bell pepper cool and then blend it with the hummus and salt in a blender or food processor, adding the water little by little until it reaches the desired consistency.

Beet Hummus

Makes ¾ to 1 cup

½ beet, peeled and diced
1 batch Basic Hummus (opposite)
Pinch of sea salt
Up to 2 tablespoons water

1. Boil the beet in water for 20 to 25 minutes.

2. Blend the beet with the hummus and salt in a blender or food processor, adding the water little by little until the hummus reaches the desired consistency.

Toasted Pine Nut Hummus

Makes 1 cup

⅓ cup pine nuts
1 batch Basic Hummus (opposite)
Up to 3 tablespoons water
Pinch of sea salt

1. Toast the pine nuts in a small pan over high heat for 2 to 3 minutes.

2. Blend about two-thirds of the toasted pine nuts with the hummus, water, and salt, adding a little more water if necessary.

3. Leave the remaining pine nuts whole or chop them if you'd like. Stir in the pine nuts with a fork.

Beet & White Bean Dip

Makes 1 cup

½ beet, peeled and diced
1 cup cooked white beans (see page 29)
⅓ cup water
⅓ cup sunflower seeds
Juice of 1 lemon
¼ teaspoon sea salt
Pinch of ground black pepper

1. Boil the beet in water for 20 to 25 minutes.

2. Blend the beet with all of the remaining ingredients in a blender or food processor until smooth.

Sunflower-Chive Cream Cheese Dip

Makes ½ cup

1 cup sunflower seeds, soaked in water (see page 29)
1 garlic clove, minced
Juice of 1 lemon
½ teaspoon sea salt
1 to 2 tablespoons water (optional)
½ handful of fresh chives

1. In a food processor, blend the sunflower seeds, garlic, lemon juice, and salt until the mixture reaches a smooth, cream cheese–like consistency.

2. Add the water if necessary and blend until the dip reaches the desired consistency. Add the chives and pulse a few times.

Smoked Paprika–Avocado Dip

Makes 1 cup

3 avocados
Handful of fresh cilantro leaves
Handful of fresh chives
¼ cup grape tomatoes
1 green onion, chopped
1 shallot, chopped
Juice of 2 limes
½ teaspoon smoked paprika
½ teaspoon sea salt
Pinch of ground black pepper

1. Pulse together all of the ingredients in a food processor. The consistency should remain fairly chunky.

Tomato Salsa

Makes 1 cup

1 cup cherry tomatoes, chopped
⅓ red onion, very finely chopped
¼ cup chopped fresh cilantro
1 green onion, chopped
Juice of 1 lime

1. Mix all of the ingredients well and store in a jar in the fridge.

Sweet and Smoky Tomato Sauce

Makes ½ cup

2 green onions, chopped
1 garlic clove, minced
2 teaspoons olive oil
¼ cup vegetable broth, or ¼ cup water mixed with ¼ teaspoon veggie bouillon paste
1 tablespoon liquid smoke
1 tablespoon maple syrup or coconut nectar
1 tablespoon tomato paste

1. Sauté the green onions and garlic in the oil in a small pot over medium heat for 3 to 4 minutes.

2. Add all of the remaining ingredients and mix well, then cook for an additional 2 minutes.

3. Remove from the stovetop and either leave as is, with a chunky consistency, or blend until smooth.

TOMATO SALSA

CHIA
PUDDINGS

Vanilla Chia Pudding with Strawberries & Cream

Makes 2 servings

Pudding
1 cup walnut milk (or any plant-based milk)
¼ cup chia seeds
2 teaspoons maple syrup
½ teaspoon vanilla extract
Pinch of sea salt

Toppings
2 tablespoons coconut cream (see Note)
2 teaspoons maple syrup (see Note)
2 strawberries, sliced

1. Mix all of the pudding ingredients thoroughly using a whisk, then store in the fridge overnight (or for at least 2 to 3 hours).

2. Mix the coconut cream with the maple syrup. Top the pudding with the cream and the strawberries and enjoy!

Note: Instead of the coconut cream, you can use aquafaba (the liquid from a can of chickpeas): Whisk ¼ cup aquafaba with 2 tablespoons maple syrup until creamy (if whisking by hand, this may take up to 10 minutes). You could also serve the pudding with plant-based yogurt instead of the coconut cream.

Chocolate-Cherry Chia Pudding

Makes 1 serving

Pudding
1 cup cashew milk
¼ cup chia seeds
1 tablespoon cacao powder
2 teaspoons maple syrup
¼ teaspoon vanilla bean
Pinch of sea salt
Pinch of cinnamon

Toppings
¼ cup frozen cherries
1 teaspoon maple syrup
¼ cup fresh pitted cherries

1. Mix all of the pudding ingredients thoroughly using a whisk, then store in the fridge overnight (or for at least 2 to 3 hours).

2. Cook the frozen cherries and maple syrup in a small pot over medium heat for 4 minutes. Top the pudding with the maple-cherry mixture and the fresh cherries.

VANILLA CHIA PUDDING WITH STRAWBERRIES & CREAM

CHOCOLATE-
CHERRY CHIA
PUDDING

OVERNIGHT
OATS

Oatmeal

½ cup quick-cooking oats

1 cup hemp milk

2 teaspoons maple syrup

¼ teaspoon vanilla extract

Pinch of sea salt

Toppings

¼ cup fresh berries of your choice

2 figs, sliced

1 tablespoon almond butter

1 tablespoon sliced almonds

1. Mix all of the oatmeal ingredients thoroughly, then transfer to a jar or bowl and refrigerate overnight.

2. Add the toppings and enjoy!

Creamy

CASHEW-PAPAYA-MAPLE-PECAN

OATMEAL

MAKES 1 SERVING

¾ cup quick-cooking oats

1 cup water

½ cup cashew milk

1 tablespoon maple syrup

½ teaspoon vanilla extract

Pinch of sea salt

Toppings
½ papaya, diced

¼ cup pecans

1 teaspoon maple syrup

1. Cook the oats in the water in a small pot over high heat for 2 minutes.

2. Mix in the cashew milk, maple syrup, vanilla, and salt, then cook for 1 more minute.

3. Serve with the toppings.

Peach & Berry
PARFAIT

MAKES 1 SERVING

Berry Layer

⅓ cup unsweetened coconut
   yogurt

1 small frozen banana, cut into
   chunks

¼ cup blackberries

½ teaspoon vanilla extract

Granola Base

1 tablespoon peanut butter

¼ cup vegan granola

¼ cup quick-cooking oats
   (optional, or use additional
   granola instead)

½ cup mixed fresh berries
   of your choice

Peach Layer

¼ cup unsweetened coconut
   yogurt

½ peach, cut into very small pieces

Toppings

1 tablespoon unsweetened
   shredded coconut or coconut
   flakes

1 tablespoon goji berries

½ tablespoon cacao nibs

More fresh berries

Fresh herbs, like basil, for garnish
   (optional)

1. Blend all the ingredients for
the berry layer in a blender until
smooth.

2. Start layering the parfait by
spooning the peanut butter and
then the granola into a jar or
glass. Add the berry mixture to
the glass, followed by the oats (or
more granola) and fresh berries.

3. Using a fork or a whisk, mix
the coconut yogurt with the peach
pieces (or blend them together in
a blender) and add the peach layer
to the glass.

4. Add the toppings and enjoy!

PEANUT BUTTER, BLUEBERRY & CHIA PARFAIT
(PAGE 216)

PEACH & BERRY PARFAIT

Peanut Butter, BLUEBERRY & CHIA PARFAIT

MAKES 1 SERVING

....

1 cup almond-soy yogurt

2 to 3 tablespoons chia seeds

2 teaspoons brown rice syrup

1 ripe banana (room temperature)

1 tablespoon peanut butter

1 frozen banana

¼ cup almond milk

1 tablespoon cacao powder

½ handful of fresh blueberries

1 teaspoon hemp seeds

1. Mix together the yogurt, chia seeds, and brown rice syrup. If possible, refrigerate for at least 1 hour, or up to overnight.

2. Slice half of the ripe banana. Fill a jar with the chia-yogurt mix, sliced banana, and then the peanut butter.

3. Blend the remaining ½ ripe banana, the frozen banana, almond milk, and cacao powder in a blender. Pour the banana mixture into the jar.

4. Top the parfait with the blueberries and hemp seeds.

Pumpkin Spice
GRANOLA

MAKES ABOUT 5 SERVINGS

1¼ cups quick-cooking oats

⅓ cup raisins

⅓ cup walnuts, chopped

¼ cup pecans, chopped

¼ cup cashews

2 tablespoons sliced almonds

2 tablespoons ground flaxseed

1 tablespoon hemp seeds

⅓ cup maple syrup

1 tablespoon pumpkin pie spice
   (or equal parts cinnamon,
   ginger, nutmeg, and cloves)

¼ teaspoon vanilla extract

1. Preheat the oven to 300°F/ 150°C.

2. Mix all of the ingredients in a bowl, making sure everything is coated with the maple syrup.

3. Spread the granola on an ungreased baking sheet and bake for 20 minutes.

4. Let cool, and then store in an airtight container at room temperature for up to 2 months.

Chocolate, COCONUT & CRANBERRY GRANOLA

MAKES ABOUT 5 SERVINGS

1 cup quick-cooking oats

⅓ cup roasted unsalted peanuts

⅓ cup unsweetened coconut shreds

⅓ cup coconut nectar

¼ cup unsweetened dried cranberries

¼ cup ground flaxseed

2 tablespoons sliced almonds

2 tablespoons cacao powder

1 tablespoon chia seeds

Pinch of sea salt

1. Preheat the oven to 300°F/ 150°C.

2. Mix all of the ingredients in a bowl, making sure everything is coated with the coconut nectar.

3. Spread the granola on an ungreased baking sheet, then bake for 20 minutes.

4. Let cool and then store in an airtight container at room temperature.

TOFU
SCRAMBLE
with Avocado

MAKES 2 SERVINGS

12 ounces extra-firm tofu

2 shallots, thinly sliced

1 green onion, chopped

1 garlic clove, minced

2 teaspoons olive oil

½ red bell pepper, chopped

1 fresh hot red chile pepper, minced (optional)

¼ teaspoon ground turmeric

¼ teaspoon kala namak

⅛ teaspoon paprika

Dash of sea salt

4 corn tortillas

Pinch of ground black pepper

Fresh cilantro, for garnish

Grape tomatoes, halved, for garnish

½ avocado, sliced, for garnish

1. Remove excess liquid from the tofu using a kitchen towel.

2. Sauté the shallots, green onion, and garlic in the oil in a pan over medium heat for 3 minutes.

3. Add the tofu, bell pepper, chile (if using), turmeric, kala namak, and salt and cook for 5 minutes, scrambling with a fork.

4. Heat the tortillas, if desired. Fill the tortillas with the scramble.

5. To serve, sprinkle the tacos with black pepper and garnish with cilantro, tomatoes, and the avocado.

CHICKPEA FLOUR

OMELET

WITH MUSHROOMS

MAKES 1 OMELET

1 tablespoon ground flaxseed

½ cup plus 2½ tablespoons water

⅓ cup chickpea flour

2 teaspoons nutritional yeast

½ teaspoon cornstarch

¼ teaspoon baking powder

¼ teaspoon dehydrated onion flakes

¼ teaspoon garlic powder, or 1 garlic clove, minced

¼ teaspoon kala namak

⅛ teaspoon ground turmeric

Pinch of sea salt

3 mushrooms, thinly sliced

Fresh chives, chopped

Pinch of ground black pepper

2 teaspoons olive oil

½ cup arugula

5 grape or cherry tomatoes, sliced

Fresh parsley, chopped

2 tablespoons barbecue sauce (optional)

1. Mix the flaxseed and 2½ tablespoons of the water in a small bowl and let sit for 3 to 5 minutes. Mix the chickpea flour, nutritional yeast, cornstarch, baking powder, onion flakes, garlic powder, kala namak, turmeric, and salt thoroughly in a large bowl.

2. Mixing constantly, add the flaxseed mixture and the remaining ½ cup water little by little to the dry ingredients. Add the mushrooms, chives, and pepper.

3. Heat the oil in a pan over medium heat. Pour in the omelet batter and cook for 5 minutes on the first side. Flip and cook for 3 minutes on the other side.

4. To serve, fill the omelet with the arugula, tomatoes, parsley, and barbecue sauce, if using.

Cherry PANCAKES

¼ cup regular or gluten-free all-purpose flour

1 tablespoon cornstarch

1 tablespoon ground flaxseed

1 teaspoon baking powder

Pinch of sea salt

¾ cup soy milk

3 tablespoons maple syrup, plus more for serving

2 tablespoons coconut oil

2 teaspoons apple cider vinegar

¼ teaspoon vanilla extract

2 teaspoons olive oil

1 tablespoon unsweetened shredded coconut, for serving

Fresh cherries or other fruit, for serving

1. Mix the flour, cornstarch, flaxseed, baking powder, and salt together in a bowl.

2. In a separate bowl, mix the soy milk, maple syrup, coconut oil, vinegar, and vanilla.

3. Combine the wet and dry mixtures and whisk together thoroughly.

4. Heat the oil in a skillet over medium heat, then scoop 2 to 3 tablespoons of batter per pancake into the skillet. Cook on each side until brown.

5. Serve with the coconut, cherries, and additional maple syrup.

Breakfast
MUFFINS

MAKES 12 TO 15 MUFFINS

2 tablespoons ground flaxseed

6 tablespoons hot water

1½ cups regular or gluten-free all-purpose flour

½ cup buckwheat flour

3 tablespoons coconut sugar

2 tablespoons quick-cooking oats

1 tablespoon baking powder

½ teaspoon sea salt

¼ teaspoon baking soda

¼ teaspoon ground cinnamon

1 cup cashew milk

½ cup plant-based yogurt

⅓ cup maple syrup

¼ cup coconut oil, melted

2 teaspoons apple cider vinegar

1 teaspoon vanilla extract

1 cup frozen or fresh wild blueberries or raspberries

½ cup chopped pecans

1. Preheat the oven to 375°F/190°C. Line a muffin pan with paper liners.

2. Combine the flaxseed and hot water and set aside for 3 minutes. Mix the flours, coconut sugar, oats, baking powder, salt, baking soda, and cinnamon in a bowl.

3. In a separate bowl, mix together the cashew milk, yogurt, maple syrup, oil, vinegar, and vanilla. Mix the wet ingredients into the dry ingredients. Don't overmix.

4. Stir in the berries and pecans.

5. Fill the muffin pan with the batter. Bake for about 25 minutes. Let cool and enjoy!

AVOCADO
TOAST

SERVES 1

3 slices regular or gluten-free sandwich bread

1 avocado, peeled and pitted

Juice of ½ lemon

1 teaspoon onion flakes

½ teaspoon garlic powder

¼ teaspoon crushed red pepper flakes

½ shallot, chopped

½ handful of chopped fresh cilantro leaves

½ handful of chopped fresh chives

½ cup grape tomatoes, sliced

Dash of paprika

Dash of sea salt

Dash of ground black pepper

1. Toast the bread to your liking.

2. While the bread toasts, place the avocado, lemon juice, onion flakes, garlic powder, and crushed red pepper flakes in a bowl, then mash together.

3. Spread the mixture over the toasted bread, then top with the shallot, cilantro, chives, tomatoes, paprika, salt, and pepper and enjoy!

Vanilla FRENCH TOAST

MAKES 2 SERVINGS

½ cup soy milk

¼ cup aquafaba (the liquid from a can of chickpeas)

¼ teaspoon vanilla extract

⅛ teaspoon kala namak

⅛ teaspoon ground turmeric

⅛ teaspoon ground cinnamon

Pinch of sea salt

6 slices regular or gluten-free sandwich bread

1 tablespoon coconut oil

Toppings

Handful of strawberries

2 tablespoons maple syrup

1. Combine the soy milk, aquafaba, vanilla, kala namak, turmeric, cinnamon, and salt in a bowl, being sure to whisk together thoroughly.

2. Soak the bread in the soy milk mixture for 3 to 5 minutes, making sure to coat each piece thoroughly and evenly.

3. Heat the oil in a pan over medium to high heat until it coats the pan, then cook the soaked bread for 2 minutes on each side, until browned.

4. Serve topped with the strawberries and maple syrup.

PAPAYA
BOATS

WITH VANILLA ICE CREAM & RAISINS

MAKES 2 SERVINGS

2 frozen bananas, cut into chunks

¼ cup almond milk

1 teaspoon vanilla extract

1 medium papaya, cut in half, seeds removed

⅓ cup raisins

Finely shredded unsweetened coconut, for garnish

1. Blend the banana, almond milk, and vanilla in a blender until smooth (depending on whether you're using a high-speed blender or not, you may need to add a little more liquid).

2. Fill the papaya boats with the raisins. Scoop the ice cream from the blender into the papaya boats, then sprinkle with coconut and enjoy!

Smoky BELL PEPPER QUINOA BOWL

MAKES 2 SERVINGS

½ cup uncooked red quinoa

1½ cups water

2 small or 1 large zucchini

2 red bell peppers

2 garlic cloves

1 cup canned full-fat coconut milk

3 tablespoons dried onion flakes

2 teaspoons smoked paprika

1 teaspoon paprika

Sea salt and ground black pepper, to taste

1½ cups grape tomatoes, halved

8 sun-dried tomatoes (preferably oil free), chopped

¼ cup fresh oregano leaves, for garnish

1. Rinse the quinoa. Combine it with the water in a large pot and simmer for about 10 minutes. Add a little more water if the quinoa looks too dry.

2. Meanwhile, dice or chop the zucchini and bell peppers and mince the garlic.

3. Reduce the heat to medium and add the zucchini, bell peppers, garlic, coconut milk, onion flakes, smoked paprika, paprika, and salt and pepper. Cook over low to medium heat for 5 minutes.

4. Add the grape tomatoes and sun-dried tomatoes and let simmer for 5 more minutes.

5. Stir well and add more seasonings if desired. Serve garnished with the oregano.

Baked
MUSTARD-TOFU
SANDWICH

MAKES 2 SANDWICHES

2 shallots, sliced

2 teaspoons olive oil

6 ounces prebaked tofu, cut into ½-inch slices (see Note)

1 teaspoon liquid smoke

1 cup fresh spinach leaves

1 pinch sea salt

2 teaspoons mustard

1 teaspoon coconut nectar

4 slices regular or gluten-free sandwich bread

¼ cup watercress

⅓ cup grape tomatoes, halved

1. Sauté the shallots in the oil in a pan over high heat for 2 minutes.

2. Add the prebaked tofu and liquid smoke to the pan and cook over medium heat for 5 more minutes. Add the spinach, season with the salt, and cook for 1 more minute.

3. Mix the mustard and coconut nectar together to make "honey mustard."

4. Spread the bread slices with the "honey mustard" and sandwich with the tofu, watercress, and grape tomatoes.

Note: Most grocery stores sell prebaked tofu in the same section as the regular tofu. But if you can't find it, you can make your own: Cut extra-firm tofu into slices and bake on a parchment paper–lined baking sheet at 400°F for 20 to 25 minutes.

Chickpea "TUNA" SANDWICHES

MAKES 4 SANDWICHES OR WRAPS

2 cups cooked chickpeas
(see page 29)

½ red onion, chopped

1 green onion, chopped

½ handful of fresh chives

Juice of 1 lemon

1 to 2 tablespoons toasted and
shredded nori (see Note)

1 tablespoon vegan mayo
(or 2 teaspoons tahini)

2 teaspoons apple cider vinegar

½ teaspoon garlic powder
(or 1 clove, minced)

Pinch of sea salt

4 regular or gluten-free wraps
or 8 slices of regular or
gluten-free sandwich bread

1 tomato, diced

½ cup arugula

½ cup fresh spinach leaves

1. Add the chickpeas, red onion, green onion, chives, lemon juice, nori, mayo, vinegar, garlic powder, and salt to a food processor and pulse until still fairly chunky. If you don't have a food processor, you can use a fork to mash the chickpeas and then just stir the ingredients together.

2. Spread the chickpea mixture on the wraps or bread and top with the tomato and greens. Roll up the wraps or close up the sandwiches.

Note: Nori is a kind of seaweed usually used for sushi. To toast it, hold it with tongs over the flame of your burner for a few seconds.

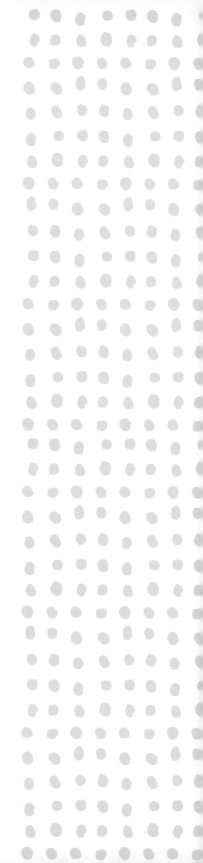

Roasted
BUTTERNUT-CARROT
SOUP

MAKES 2 SERVINGS

¼ butternut squash, with the skin, seeds removed, diced

2 carrots, chopped

½ cup canned full-fat coconut milk

¼ cup vegetable broth

Pinch of sea salt

2 cups shredded kale

1 teaspoon olive oil

Pinch of ground black pepper

½ handful of fresh parsley leaves, for garnish

2 tablespoons sunflower seeds

1. Preheat the oven to 400°F/ 200°C. Line a baking sheet with parchment paper.

2. Spread the squash and carrots on the baking sheet and bake for 45 minutes.

3. Blend the squash, carrots, coconut milk, broth, and salt in a blender or using an immersion blender until smooth.

4. Transfer the soup to a pot, set over medium heat, and cook for 3 minutes. Add the kale and cook for an additional 2 minutes.

5. Serve drizzled with the olive oil and sprinkled with the pepper, parsley, and sunflower seeds.

ZUCCHINI-POTATO
SOUP
(PAGE 242)

ROASTED BUTTERNUT-
CARROT SOUP

ZUCCHINI-POTATO

Soup

MAKES 2 SERVINGS

2 medium potatoes, diced

1 zucchini, chopped

1 cup vegetable broth, or 1 cup water mixed with 1 teaspoon veggie bouillon paste

2 tablespoons nutritional yeast

1 slice regular or gluten-free bread, toasted, cut in half

1 teaspoon olive oil

2 tablespoons pumpkin seeds

Pinch of crushed red pepper flakes

Pinch of ground black pepper

1. Boil the potatoes in water for 25 minutes. Drain.

2. In a separate pot, cook the zucchini in the broth over high heat for 5 minutes.

3. Blend the zucchini, broth, potatoes, and nutritional yeast in a blender or with an immersion blender until smooth.

4. Drizzle the toast with the olive oil. Serve the soup with the toasts on the side and garnish the soup with the pumpkin seeds, red pepper flakes, and black pepper.

Creamy
ZUCCHINI NOODLE
SALAD

WITH WALNUTS

MAKES 2 SERVINGS

10 sun-dried tomatoes, chopped

2 cups cremini mushrooms

Juice of 1 lemon

2 large zucchini

1 avocado, peeled and pit removed

1 mango, peeled and pitted

Handful of fresh basil leaves

½ handful of fresh cilantro leaves, chopped

2 green onions, chopped

Juice of 1 lime

1 cup cherry or grape tomatoes, halved

½ cup walnuts, chopped

½ handful of fresh chives, chopped

Extra herbs of your choice, to garnish

1. If your sun-dried tomatoes are oil-free, soak them in a cup of water for at least 20 minutes. If they're not oil-free, remove excess oil using a paper towel and skip the soaking. If you can't find salt-free sun-dried tomatoes, add them to the dish at the very end.

2. Slice the mushrooms thinly. Toss them with the lemon juice in a bowl and let them sit for 20 to 30 minutes.

3. Spiralize the zucchini using a spiralizer or a julienne vegetable peeler.

4. In a blender or food processor, blend the avocado, mango, basil, cilantro, half the green onions, and the lime juice.

5. In a bowl, mix the zucchini noodles with the dressing and add the cherry tomatoes.

6. Toast the walnuts in a nonstick pan over medium heat for about 4 minutes.

7. Drain the mushrooms and sun-dried tomatoes (if necessary) and add them to the zucchini noodles. Serve the salad garnished with the chives, the remaining green onions, and the extra herbs. Top with the toasted walnuts.

Creamy
ALMOND &
HEARTS OF PALM
SALAD

MAKES 2 SERVINGS

Dressing

⅓ cup blanched almonds, soaked
 in water (see page 29)

¼ cup water

¼ cup nutritional yeast

Juice of 1 lemon

2 tablespoons olive oil

1 teaspoon apple cider vinegar

¼ teaspoon sea salt

Salad

2 medium heads romaine lettuce,
 chopped

1 cup cherry tomatoes, halved

1 bell pepper, chopped

1 celery stalk, very finely chopped

1 can hearts of palm, cut into
 ½-inch pieces

1 green onion, chopped

4 sun-dried tomatoes, chopped

Toppings

2 almonds, grated

1 teaspoon hemp seeds

1. Blend all of the dressing
ingredients in a blender until
smooth.

2. Mix all of the salad ingredients
in a large bowl and toss with the
dressing.

3. Top with the almonds and
hemp seeds and enjoy.

Note: If you're preparing this in
advance, be sure to store the dressing
separately and only mix it when you're
about to eat the salad.

CREAMY ALMOND & HEARTS OF PALM SALAD

CREAMY ZUCCHINI NOODLE SALAD WITH WALNUTS (PAGE 243)

GRAPEFRUIT-PISTACHIO
Salad

MAKES 2 SERVINGS

2 cups cooked millet (see How to Cook Quinoa, page 29)

1 cucumber, chopped

2 green onions, finely chopped

Sea salt and ground black pepper, to taste

2 grapefruits, zested (for 2 teaspoons zest), peeled, and diced

4 cups arugula

3 tablespoons balsamic vinegar

⅓ cup chopped pistachios

1. Mix the millet with the cucumber and green onions and season with salt and pepper.

2. Serve the millet mixture and diced grapefruit on a bed of the arugula.

3. Dress with the vinegar and top with the pistachios and grapefruit zest.

AVOCADO-KALE
SALAD
WITH BUTTERNUT & SWEET POTATO

MAKES 2 SERVINGS

½ butternut squash, seeds removed, cut into 1-inch pieces

1 teaspoon olive oil, plus more for drizzling over the squash

¼ teaspoon sea salt plus 1 pinch

1 large avocado

4 cups shredded curly kale

1 collard green leaf, chopped

¼ cup pumpkin seeds

¼ teaspoon curry powder

¼ teaspoon crushed red pepper flakes

1. Preheat the oven to 350°F/ 177°C. Line a baking sheet with parchment paper. Spread the squash on the baking sheet, drizzle with oil, and sprinkle with a pinch of salt. Bake for 45 minutes.

2. In a large bowl, massage the avocado into the kale and collard greens. Add the butternut squash.

3. Toast the pumpkin seeds in the remaining 1 teaspoon oil in a skillet over high heat for 1 minute. Reduce the heat to medium, add the curry powder, red pepper flakes, and remaining ¼ teaspoon salt, and toast for 1 to 2 more minutes. Sprinkle the seeds over the salad.

Coconut & Kale
RICE NOODLE
BOWL

MAKES 2 SERVINGS, OR 4 AS A SNACK

1 sweet potato, peeled and diced

1 large or 2 small onions, chopped

2 garlic cloves, minced

2 cups vegetable broth, or 2 cups water mixed with 2 teaspoons veggie bouillon paste

2 celery stalks, chopped

1 to 2 teaspoons grated fresh ginger

1 cup canned full-fat coconut milk

½ cup dried yellow lentils

1 to 2 teaspoons Thai curry paste (depending on how spicy you want it to be)

½ teaspoon paprika

¼ teaspoon ground turmeric

2 ounces dried glass noodles

2 cups chopped kale

Pinch of ground black pepper

Handful of fresh herbs, such as cilantro or Thai basil leaves

1. Put the sweet potato, onion, garlic, and 1 cup of the broth in a pot and bring to a boil. Reduce the heat to medium as soon as it starts boiling, and cook for about 5 minutes.

2. Add the celery and ginger to the pot. Lower the heat to medium-low and cook, covered, for 5 more minutes.

3. Add the remaining 1 cup broth, the coconut milk, lentils, curry paste, paprika, and turmeric. Cook for 10 minutes.

4. Add the noodles and kale and cook for 5 more minutes over low heat, stirring well so it doesn't burn. Add more water if necessary, but not too much.

5. Serve the soup sprinkled with the pepper and fresh herbs.

Walnut-Basil

PASTA

MAKES 2 SERVINGS

1 red onion, sliced

1 green onion, chopped

2 garlic cloves, minced

1 tablespoon olive oil

2 large tomatoes, diced

½ cup walnuts, chopped

2 teaspoons sun-dried tomato paste (see Note)

2 teaspoons tomato paste (see Note)

½ teaspoon dried Italian herbs

½ teaspoon sea salt

Handful of fresh basil leaves, plus more for garnish

2 pitted Medjool dates, chopped

6 ounces dried regular or gluten-free spaghetti

Cherry tomatoes, halved, for garnish

1. In a large pan, sauté the red onion, green onion, and garlic in the oil over medium heat for 5 minutes.

2. Add the tomatoes, walnuts, tomato pastes, Italian herbs, and salt to the pan and cook for 5 more minutes. The tomatoes should add enough liquid, but feel free to add a few tablespoons of water or vegetable broth if necessary. Add the fresh basil last.

3. Transfer to a food processor and pulse the sauce with the dates (you can omit this step if you chop the dates very finely and simply add them to the pan).

4. Cook the pasta according to package instructions. Serve topped with the sauce, and garnish with more fresh basil and a few halved cherry tomatoes.

Note: Instead of using the sun-dried tomato paste, you can use ⅓ cup chopped sun-dried tomatoes and increase the regular tomato paste to 1 tablespoon.

Creamy
MUSHROOM
PENNE

MAKES 2 SERVINGS

Mushrooms & Pasta

1 cup cremini mushrooms, thinly sliced

1 cup shiitake mushrooms, stems discarded, thinly sliced

1 cup white button mushrooms, thinly sliced

1 shallot, chopped

1 garlic clove, minced

1 tablespoon olive oil

6 ounces dried regular or gluten-free penne

Note: Brush or peel the mushrooms to clean them, but don't wash them.

Sauce

1 cup vegetable broth, or 1 cup water mixed with 1 teaspoon veggie bouillon paste

½ cup cashews, soaked in water (see page 29)

1 tablespoon nutritional yeast

1 tablespoon olive oil

Juice of ½ lemon

Pinch of sea salt

Pinch of ground black pepper

½ teaspoon dried basil

6 sun-dried tomatoes

1 tablespoon fresh oregano leaves

1. Sauté all of the mushrooms, the shallot, and garlic in the oil in a large pan over medium heat for 7 minutes.

2. Bring a pot of water to a boil and cook the pasta according to the package instructions.

3. To make the sauce, blend ¾ cup of the broth, the cashews, nutritional yeast, oil, lemon juice, salt, and pepper in a blender until smooth.

4. Add the sauce, dried basil, and remaining ¼ cup broth to the pan with the mushrooms, stir well, and lower the heat to low. Cook for another 3 minutes.

5. Serve the pasta with the mushroom-sauce mixture, sun-dried tomatoes, and oregano.

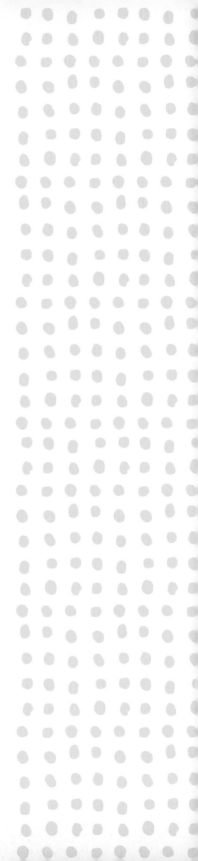

SPINACH
PASTA

WITH ZUCCHINI-NUT SAUCE

MAKES 2 SERVINGS

Pasta

6 ounces dried regular or gluten-free fettuccine

4 cups baby spinach

½ cup grape tomatoes, halved

Pinch of ground black pepper

Sauce

1 cup water

½ cup blanched almonds, soaked in water (see page 29), or ¾ cup sliced almonds

½ small zucchini (peeled or unpeeled)

¼ cup pine nuts

Juice of 1 lime

1 or 2 garlic cloves, peeled

1 tablespoon onion flakes

2 teaspoons cornstarch

1 teaspoon grated nutmeg

½ teaspoon sea salt

1. Bring a pot of water to a boil and cook the pasta according to the package instructions.

2. Meanwhile, blend all of the sauce ingredients in a blender until smooth. Transfer to a pot and cook the sauce over high heat for 2 minutes. Stir with a whisk and add ½ cup more water while cooking.

3. Reduce the heat to low and add the spinach to the sauce, then cook for 2 more minutes.

4. Serve the pasta with the sauce, tomatoes, and pepper.

Butternut or Sweet Potato

MAC 'N' CHEESE
SAUCE

MAKES 4 SERVINGS

½ butternut squash, peeled, seeds removed, and diced, or 1 large or 2 medium sweet potatoes, peeled and diced

1 cup cashews, soaked in water (see page 29)

1 cup water

⅓ cup nutritional yeast

⅓ red bell pepper, chopped

½ celery stalk, chopped

1 green onion, trimmed

¼ cup cornstarch

Juice of 1 lemon

1 tablespoon yellow mustard

1 tablespoon dried minced onion

1 garlic clove, peeled

1 teaspoon garlic powder

½ teaspoon paprika

½ teaspoon sea salt

Pinch of ground black pepper

1. Preheat the oven to 350°F/177°C. Line a baking sheet with parchment paper. Bake the squash or sweet potatoes for 45 minutes. Alternatively, boil them in water for 25 minutes.

2. Blend all of the ingredients in a high-speed blender until the sauce reaches a very smooth consistency.

3. Transfer to a pot and cook over high heat for 3 minutes, then reduce the heat to low and let the sauce simmer for 3 more minutes. Add a little liquid if necessary (cashew milk, for instance), but not too much; you want the consistency to remain very creamy.

4. Serve with your favorite pasta and top with fresh herbs or other toppings such as Shiitake Bacon (page 196), or let cool and refrigerate or freeze for later.

Note: Serve this sauce with your preferred pasta. You can keep leftover sauce in the fridge for about 5 days or in the freezer for up to 3 months.

VARIATION

Smoky Carrot Mac 'n' Cheese Sauce

Replace the squash or sweet potatoes with 2 medium potatoes and 1 carrot, both diced. Bake or boil them as directed. Add 2 tablespoons liquid smoke along with the rest of the sauce ingredients.

Chickpea
CURRY

WITH CAULIFLOWER RICE

MAKES 2 SERVINGS

Cauliflower Rice
**1 small or ½ large head cauliflower,
cut into florets**
Handful of fresh cilantro leaves
1 green onion, chopped
Juice of 1 lime

Curry
1 onion, sliced
1 red bell pepper, sliced
2 garlic cloves, sliced
1 teaspoon coconut oil
1 cup canned full-fat coconut milk
2 teaspoons veggie bouillon paste
**2 cups cooked chickpeas
(see page 29)**
½ cup cashews
1 tablespoon curry powder
**¼ fresh hot red chile pepper,
sliced**
¼ teaspoon paprika
¼ teaspoon ground coriander
¼ teaspoon sea salt
Pinch of ground black pepper
2 cups fresh spinach leaves
Fresh cilantro leaves, for garnish

1. To make the cauliflower rice, process the cauliflower in a food processor until it reaches a rice-like consistency.

2. Add the cilantro and green onion and pulse again.

3. Stir in the lime juice.

4. For the curry, sauté the onion, bell pepper, and garlic in the oil over medium heat for 5 minutes.

5. Add the coconut milk and veggie paste and stir well. Add the chickpeas, cashews, curry powder, chile, paprika, coriander, salt, and black pepper. Cook for 7 more minutes. Stir in the spinach at the very end.

6. Serve over the cauliflower rice and garnish with fresh cilantro.

Note: If you'd prefer, you can serve the curry over cooked brown rice, millet, or quinoa instead of making the cauliflower rice.

Miso-Ginger
TEMPEH BOWL
WITH BEET-TAHINI DRESSING

MAKES 1 SERVING

Cinnamon-Chile Sweet Potatoes

1 small or ½ large sweet potato, peeled and chopped into 1-inch pieces

½ tablespoon olive or coconut oil

1 teaspoon ground cinnamon

¼ fresh hot red chile pepper, minced

Pinch of sea salt

Shiitake Bacon

2 ounces fresh shiitake mushrooms, stems discarded, sliced

1 to 2 teaspoons olive or coconut oil

Pinch of sea salt

Note: The shiitake bacon in this recipe is a slightly simplified version of the version you'll find on page 196. If you'd like, you can substitute that recipe here.

Veggies

¼ head cauliflower, chopped

1 red onion, chopped

1 green onion, chopped

½ orange bell pepper, chopped

1 tablespoon olive or coconut oil

Sea salt and freshly ground black pepper, to taste

Miso-Ginger Tempeh

3 tablespoons water

2 teaspoons miso paste

1-inch piece fresh ginger, peeled and grated

2 ounces tempeh, sliced

Pink Dressing

3 tablespoons water

1 tablespoon sunflower seed butter or tahini

Juice of 1 lime

1 teaspoon beet powder

For Serving

1 cup baby spinach leaves

1. Preheat the oven to 350°F/177°C. Line a baking sheet with parchment paper.

2. Toss the sweet potato with the oil, cinnamon, chile, and salt (it'll work best if you use your hands). Spread the sweet potatoes on one side of the baking sheet and bake for 45 minutes.

3. Meanwhile, to make the shiitake bacon, mix the mushrooms with the oil and salt. After the sweet potatoes have baked for 15 to 20 minutes, add the mushrooms to the other side of the baking sheet and bake for 25 to 30 minutes, depending on how crispy you want your shiitake bacon to be.

4. For the veggies, combine the chopped vegetables with the oil in a pan and season with salt and pepper. Cook over low to medium heat for 15 to 20 minutes.

5. To make the tempeh, mix the water, miso paste, and ginger in a bowl. Add the tempeh and let it marinate for a few minutes, then heat the slices in a pan over low to medium heat for 5 to 10 minutes.

6. To make the dressing, mix all of the dressing ingredients using a fork or a whisk.

7. Serve the tempeh with the sweet potatoes, mushrooms, and veggies over the baby spinach and drizzle with the dressing.

Chili-Lime
CAULIFLOWER
BOWL

MAKES 2 SERVINGS

1 shallot, sliced

1 garlic clove, minced

⅓ head yellow cauliflower, chopped

1 bell pepper, chopped

1 tablespoon olive oil

⅓ cup whole almonds

¼ fresh hot red chile pepper, thinly sliced

⅔ cup boiling water

½ cup couscous

½ teaspoon sea salt

½ teaspoon ground cardamom

Juice of 1 lime

4 collard green leaves, chopped

2 cups chopped curly kale

Handful of fresh parsley leaves, for garnish

1. Sauté the shallot, garlic, cauliflower, and bell pepper in the oil in a pan over medium heat for 3 minutes.

2. Add the almonds and chile and cook for 5 more minutes.

3. Meanwhile, pour the boiling water over the couscous in a separate pot, add the salt, stir well, and let sit for 5 minutes. Add a little more water if the couscous looks too dry.

4. Stir the cardamom and lime juice into the couscous and transfer the couscous to the pan with the vegetables, stirring to combine.

5. Cook the collard greens and kale in a large pan with about 2 tablespoons water over high heat for 3 minutes.

6. Serve the couscous and vegetables over the greens and garnish with the parsley.

Purple Cabbage
CHICKPEA
BOATS

2 cups shiitake mushrooms

1 shallot, sliced

½ red bell pepper, diced

½ orange bell pepper, diced

1 tablespoon olive oil

1 cup cooked chickpeas
  (see page 29)

1 teaspoon ground turmeric

1 teaspoon paprika

½ teaspoon garlic powder

¼ teaspoon sea salt

4 small or 2 large purple cabbage
  leaves

2 cups arugula

1. Cook the mushrooms, shallot, and bell peppers in the olive oil in a pan set over medium heat for 5 minutes.

2. Add the chickpeas, turmeric, paprika, garlic powder, and salt and cook for 3 minutes more.

3. Fill the cabbage leaves with the chickpea mixture and serve over a bed of arugula.

Oyster Chop &
POTATO
BOWL

MAKES 1 SERVING

Potatoes

1 large potato, cut into cubes
1 tablespoon olive oil
2 teaspoons coriander seeds
½ teaspoon sea salt
½ teaspoon garlic powder
¼ teaspoon chili powder
¼ teaspoon mustard powder
Pinch of chili flakes

Mushroom chops

1 to 2 tablespoons olive oil
3 large oyster mushroom stems, cut into ½-inch "chops" (make sure they aren't too thick)
2 teaspoons liquid smoke
2 teaspoons tamari or soy sauce
Pinch of sea salt
⅓ cup shredded purple cabbage
1 cup broccoli florets

1. For the potatoes, preheat the oven to 400°F/200°C. Line a baking sheet with parchment paper.

2. Mix all of the ingredients together in a bowl, making sure the potatoes are coated thoroughly.

3. Spread the potatoes on the baking sheet and bake for 45 minutes.

4. Meanwhile, sauté the mushroom chops in the oil over medium heat for 3 minutes.

5. Add the liquid smoke, soy sauce, and salt to the pan and mix well.

6. Add the cabbage and broccoli and cook everything for 5 to 7 more minutes. Serve the mushroom mixture and the potatoes together in a bowl.

Maple-Glazed
TEMPEH

WITH SAFFRON QUINOA & STEAMED KALE

MAKES 2 SERVINGS

½ cup red quinoa

1½ cups water

½ cup vegetable broth, or ½ cup water mixed with ½ teaspoon veggie bouillon paste

8 ounces tempeh

1 onion, chopped

2 garlic cloves, minced

2 teaspoons olive oil

1 orange bell pepper, chopped

2 teaspoons liquid smoke

2 teaspoons dehydrated onion flakes

1 teaspoon tamari or soy sauce

¼ teaspoon smoked paprika

¼ teaspoon ground coriander

Pinch of sea salt

1 saffron thread

1 tablespoon maple syrup

3 cups chopped curly kale

1 green onion, chopped

4 tablespoons mustard

1. Combine the quinoa, water, and broth in a pot and bring to a boil, then reduce the heat to medium and cook for 18 minutes (set a timer).

2. Meanwhile, cut the tempeh into ½- to 1-inch pieces.

3. Sauté the onion and garlic in the oil in a pan over medium heat for 5 minutes.

4. Add the bell pepper and tempeh to the pan and sauté for 3 more minutes. Reduce the heat to low. Add the liquid smoke, onion flakes, soy sauce, smoked paprika, coriander, salt, and saffron, and cook for 5 minutes more. Add the maple syrup, mix well, and remove from the stovetop.

5. When the timer reaches minute 18, add the kale and green onion to the quinoa and cook over medium-low heat for 5 more minutes.

6. Serve the quinoa mixture with the tempeh mixture, and the mustard for dressing.

Tahini CARAMEL SAUCE

MAKES ABOUT ¼ CUP

⅓ cup coconut sugar
¼ cup water
⅓ cup tahini
¼ teaspoon sea salt

1. Mix the coconut sugar and water in a small pot. Cook over medium to high heat for 3 minutes. Don't stir too much.

2. Remove the pot from the stovetop and whisk in the tahini and salt until the caramel sauce is thick and creamy.

Chocolate Sauce
(page 274)

TAHINI CARAMEL SAUCE

CHOCOLATE
SAUCE

MAKES ABOUT ¼ CUP

⅓ cup cacao powder
⅓ cup maple syrup
¼ cup coconut oil, melted
Pinch of sea salt

1. Mix all of the ingredients together using a whisk.

Homemade
CHOCOLATE
BASE

½ cup melted cacao butter

½ cup cacao powder

3 tablespoons coconut nectar (or maple syrup)

1 teaspoon coconut oil

⅛ teaspoon vanilla extract

Pinch of sea salt

1. Mix all of the ingredients using a whisk. Pour into chocolate molds and refrigerate or freeze for at least 30 to 60 minutes before serving, or use it to make one of the chocolates on pages 276 to 278.

Salted Pistachio
CHOCOLATE

Ingredients for Homemade Chocolate Base (above)

¼ cup pistachios (chopped or whole, as you prefer)

¼ teaspoon sea salt

1. Mix all of the ingredients using a whisk. Pour into chocolate molds or spread the mixture on a parchment paper-lined baking sheet and refrigerate or freeze for at least 30 to 60 minutes before serving. If you used a baking sheet, break into individual serving pieces.

Goji Berry

CHILI

PRALINES

MAKES 6 TO 8 PRALINES, DEPENDING ON THE SIZE OF THE MOLDS

**Ingredients for Homemade
Chocolate Base (page 275)**

⅓ cup goji berries

**¼ teaspoon crushed red pepper
flakes**

1. Mix all of the ingredients using a whisk. Pour into praline molds or lined mini-muffin cups and refrigerate or freeze for at least 30 to 60 minutes before serving.

VEGAN
RESET

276

HAZELNUT
Vanilla
PRALINES

6 TO 8 PRALINES, DEPENDING ON THE SIZE OF THE MOLDS

Ingredients for Homemade Chocolate Base (page 275)
½ teaspoon vanilla bean paste
⅓ cup whole hazelnuts

1. Mix the chocolate base ingredients and vanilla paste using a whisk. Place 1 hazelnut into each praline mold or lined mini-muffin cup and then fill the molds with the chocolate. Refrigerate or freeze for at least 30 to 60 minutes before serving.

SALTED

Dark Chocolate

NUT BUTTER CUPS

MAKES ABOUT 9 NUT BUTTER CUPS

⅓ cup coconut oil

⅓ cup cocoa butter, melted

⅓ cup maple syrup

½ cup plus 2 tablespoons cacao powder

1 teaspoon vanilla extract

½ teaspoon sea salt, plus a little more for sprinkling

3 to 4 teaspoons cashew butter

3 to 4 teaspoons peanut butter

3 to 4 teaspoons almond butter

1. To make the chocolate, mix together the coconut oil, cocoa butter, maple syrup, cacao powder, vanilla, and salt in a bowl using a whisk.

2. Add about 2 teaspoons of the melted chocolate mix to each of 9 cupcake forms. Refrigerate or freeze for 10 minutes.

3. Add a little more than 1 teaspoon nut butter to each form.

4. Cover with more chocolate, sprinkle a little sea salt on top, and refrigerate or freeze for another 20 minutes before serving.

Double Chocolate
BROWNIES

MAKES 6 BROWNIES

2 tablespoons ground flaxseed

6 tablespoons water

1 cup cooked chickpeas
   (see page 29)

½ cup coconut milk (the kind
   in a carton, for drinking, not
   canned)

½ cup almond butter

½ cup cacao powder

⅓ cup maple syrup

3 tablespoons coconut sugar

1 teaspoon baking powder

¼ teaspoon baking soda

¼ teaspoon sea salt

½ cup vegan chocolate
   chips (optional but highly
   recommended)

1. Preheat the oven to 350°F/ 177°C. Line a 7- x 5- x 1½-inch baking pan or other similar-size baking dish with parchment paper.

2. Combine the flaxseed and water and let sit for 3 minutes.

3. Place chickpeas, coconut milk, almond butter, cacao powder, maple syrup, coconut sugar, baking powder, baking soda, salt, and the flaxseed mixture in a food processor or blender and process until smooth.

4. Stir in the chocolate chips, if using, with a spoon and transfer the batter to the prepared baking pan. Bake for 35 minutes. These are best eaten immediately or within 1 to 2 days. To store, let cool completely and then refrigerate in an airtight container for up to 1 week, or freeze up to 1 month.

Notes: The baking time may vary depending on the size of the pan you're using. You can also double the recipe and use a larger pan, which will also affect the baking time.

Feel free to add ½ cup chopped walnuts or any nuts you like to the batter.

Red Velvet
TRUFFLES

MAKES ABOUT 20 TRUFFLES

Truffles

1 cup unsweetened finely shredded coconut

¾ cup ground almonds

¼ cup beet root powder

3 tablespoons maple syrup

2 tablespoons white almond butter

2 tablespoons coconut butter, melted

2 teaspoons cacao powder

White Chocolate–Coconut Coating

½ cup melted cacao butter

¼ cup coconut butter

2 tablespoons maple syrup

1 cup unsweetened finely shredded coconut

1. Pulse all of the truffle ingredients in a food processor until the mixture reaches a dough-like consistency (if it's too crumbly, add some more almond butter or maple syrup).

2. Use your hands to form the dough into 1-inch truffles. Place the truffles in a container and put them in the freezer for 10 to 15 minutes while you make the white chocolate coating.

3. For the coating, melt the cacao butter and coconut butter in a small pan (be careful not to burn them).

4. Transfer the melted butters to a bowl and mix in the maple syrup using a whisk. Let the mixture cool for a few minutes.

5. Using toothpicks or your hands, coat the truffles with the white chocolate mixture one by one and then roll them in the shredded coconut.

6. Refrigerate or freeze the truffles for about 10 minutes before serving.

Avocado-Chocolate
MOUSSE

MAKES 4 SERVINGS
....

2 small to medium ripe avocados
½ cup cacao powder
½ cup chocolate chips, melted
½ cup maple syrup
¼ cup plant-based milk of choice
Pinch of sea salt
Fresh mixed berries, for serving
**A few sprigs fresh mint, for
    serving**

1. Blend the avocados, cacao powder, chocolate chips, maple syrup, plant-based milk, and salt in a blender until smooth.

2. To serve, place some berries in parfait glasses, add the mousse, and garnish with mint leaves.

Note: This mousse should be eaten soon after it's made, so be sure to prepare it as close to serving time as possible. Keep the mousse refrigerated until you're ready to serve.

Apple-Cinnamon
CRUMBLE
WITH COCONUT CREAM

MAKES 4 TO 6 SERVINGS

Apple Crumble
⅓ cup walnuts
⅓ cup pecans
1 cup pitted Medjool dates
2 teaspoons ground cinnamon
1 teaspoon vanilla extract
Pinch of sea salt
2 apples, diced

Coconut Cream
1 can full-fat coconut cream, chilled in the fridge overnight
3 tablespoons maple syrup

1. Preheat the oven to 350°F/ 177°C.

2. Place the nuts and dates in a food processor and add the cinnamon, vanilla, and salt. Pulse until crumbly.

3. Mix in the diced apples, transfer to a baking dish, and bake for 15 minutes.

4. Drain the liquid from the chilled coconut cream and use the solid part only. Mix the solid coconut cream and maple syrup using a whisk or blender.

5. Serve the crumble with the cream.

Espresso & White Chocolate
CASHEW MOUSSE

MAKES 6 SERVINGS

White Chocolate Layer

1 cup cashews, soaked in water (see page 29)

⅔ cup coconut water

½ cup pitted Medjool dates

¼ cup cacao butter, melted

Juice of 1 lemon

1 teaspoon vanilla extract

Pinch of sea salt

Mocha Layer

1 cup cashews, soaked in water (see page 29)

⅓ cup maple syrup

¼ cup coconut water

¼ cup brewed espresso, chilled

¼ cup cacao powder

Pinch of sea salt

1. Blend all of the ingredients for the white chocolate layer in a high-speed blender or food processor until smooth.

2. Blend all of the ingredients for the mocha layer in a high-speed blender or food processor until smooth.

3. Layer the white chocolate and the mocha layers in jars and refrigerate them for a few hours, or freeze for 30 to 40 minutes, before serving.

Appendix &
RESOURCES

WHAT TO EAT INSTEAD

Meat

Tofu

Tempeh

Seitan

Jackfruit

Mushrooms

Legumes

Honey

Blackstrap molasses

Brown rice syrup

Coconut nectar

Maple syrup

Cheese

There are many store-bought vegan cheese options, or you can make homemade "cheesy" sauces using some of the recipes in this book. Nutritional yeast and nuts are common ingredients used to create a cheesy flavor.

Eggs

(The measurements are the equivalent of one egg used for cooking or baking.)

1 tablespoon ground flaxseed + 3 tablespoons water

¼ cup unsweetened applesauce

1 tablespoon chia seeds + ⅓ cup water

1 tablespoon agar-agar + 1 tablespoon water

½ to 1 ripe banana, mashed

3 tablespoons peanut butter

2 tablespoons aquafaba (the liquid from canned chickpeas)

Butter

Unrefined coconut oil

Vegan butter or margarine

Olive oil (keep in mind the flavor is less neutral than coconut oil)

Mashed avocado

Unsweetened applesauce

Sugar

Organic sugar

Dates

Molasses

Maple syrup

Brown rice syrup

Coconut sugar

Coconut nectar

Applesauce

Bananas (or any other sweet fruit)

WHAT TO DRINK INSTEAD

Milk

Coconut milk (the type in cartons, not cans)

Oat milk

Hemp milk

Rice milk

Walnut milk

Soy milk

Hazelnut milk

Almond milk

Brazil nut milk

Cashew milk

WHAT TO WEAR INSTEAD

Faux leather

Cotton

Linen

Synthetic material such as polyester, nylon, acrylic, and rayon

Faux suede

Cork

Microfiber

WHAT TO DO INSTEAD

- Instead of heading to the zoo, where animals are held in captivity, visit and support your closest animal sanctuary or wildlife rescue center.

- Instead of a circus that exploits animals, visit one of the many animal-free circuses that are steadily growing in popularity.

VEGAN RESOURCES

I keep an up-to-date list of vegan brands, websites, books, and documentaries online at VeganReset.com. Here are a few of my personal favorite websites, books, and documentaries.

Websites

carnism.org

farmusa.org (Farm Animal Rights Movement)

mercyforanimals.org

peta.org

sanctuaries.org

vegan.com

vegansociety.com

vegnews.com

vegsource.com

bestofvegan.com

veganhealth.org

theveganrd.com

nutritionfacts.org

Documentaries

Blackfish

Cowspiracy

The Cove

Earthlings

Fat, Sick & Nearly Dead

Forks Over Knives

May I Be Frank

Vegucated

Books

Beg: A Radical New Way of Regarding Animals by Rory Freedman

Breaking the Food Seduction: The Hidden Reasons Behind Food Cravings and 7 Steps to End Them Naturally by Neal D. Barnard

The China Study: The Most Comprehensive Study of Nutrition Ever Conducted and the Startling Implications for Diet, Weight Loss and Long-Term Health by Thomas Campbell and T. Colin Campbell

Dr. Neal Barnard's Program for Reversing Diabetes: The Scientifically Proven System for Reversing Diabetes without Drugs by Neal D. Barnard

Eating Animals by Jonathan Safran Foer

Eat to Live by Joel Fuhrman

How Not to Die by Dr. Michael Greger

The Kind Diet: A Simple Guide to Feeling Great, Losing Weight, and Saving the Planet by Alicia Silverstone

Muzzling a Movement: The Effects of Anti-Terrorism Law, Money, and Politics on Animal Activism by Dara Lovitz

Power Foods for the Brain: An Effective 3-Step Plan to Protect Your Mind and Strengthen Your Memory by Neal D. Barnard

Prevent and Reverse Heart Disease: The Revolutionary, Scientifically Proven, Nutrition-Based Cure by Caldwell B. Esselstyn, Jr.

Sistah Vegan: Food, Identity, Health, and Society: Black Female Vegans Speak by A. Breeze Harper (editor)

Slaughterhouse: The Shocking Story of Greed, Neglect, and Inhumane Treatment Inside the U.S. Meat Industry by Gail Eisnitz

Vegan for Her: The Woman's Guide to Being Healthy and Fit on a Plant-Based Diet by Virginia Messina and JL Fields

Vegan for Life: Everything You Need to Know to Be Healthy and Fit on a Plant-Based Diet by Jack Norris and Virginia Messina

Whole: Rethinking the Science of Nutrition by T. Colin Campbell

Why We Love Dogs, Eat Pigs, and Wear Cows: An Introduction to Carnism by Melanie Joy

Plant-based foods that are rich in protein

Lentils

Tofu

Black beans

Quinoa

Amaranth

Soy milk

Black-eyed peas

Broccoli

Asparagus

Green beans

Almonds

Spirulina

Green peas

Hemp seeds

Oats

Pumpkin seeds

Chia seeds

Tempeh

Tahini

Nutritional yeast

Spinach

Chickpeas

Peanut butter

Plant-based foods that are rich in calcium

Kale

Collard greens

Blackstrap molasses

Tempeh

Turnip greens

Fortified nondairy milk

Hemp milk

Fortified orange juice (just make sure it doesn't contain vitamin D_3 derived from animal products)

Tahini

Almond butter

Great northern beans

Soybeans

Broccoli

Fennel

Blackberries

Black currants

Oranges

Dried apricots

Figs

Dates

Artichokes

Sesame seeds

Adzuki beans

Navy beans

Amaranth

Vitamin B_{12}

Getting enough Vitamin B_{12} is important for healthy brain and nervous system functioning. Although there are some good vegan sources such as nutritional yeast, spirulina, and seaweed, I recommend you take a supplement. Here are some important things to know about B_{12}:

- The water-soluble vitamin B_{12} is actually a bacteria produced by microorganisms and it can be found in the soil where fruit trees and vegetables grow. One of the ways people used to get their supply of B_{12} was by eating unwashed fruits and vegetables. But I wouldn't advise relying on that as your only source, since you'd never be sure how much you are actually getting.

- While it is true that animal products contain B_{12}, they often get it because their food is enriched with B_{12} supplements.

- B_{12} is stored in the body for years, so if you were to become deficient, you wouldn't notice any symptoms for at least a couple of years. You can have your doctor test your blood to find out if you have a B_{12} deficiency.

Vitamin D

The best source of vitamin D is exposure to sunlight. If you can, get at least a bit of daily sunlight; otherwise, you can get your vitamin D from fortified plant-based milks or by taking a Vitamin D_2 or D_3 supplement (be sure to choose a supplement that is vegan).

Omega-3 Fatty Acids

You might have heard that omega-3 fatty acids are good for you, but what is equally important is the ratio of omega-3 to omega-6 fatty acids. Some experts say it should be 1:4; others say it should be closer to 1:1. Here are some foods that are high in omega-3 fatty acids but not in omega-6:

Flaxseed
Chia seeds
Hemp seeds
Mustard oil
Seaweed
Beans
Winter squash
Leafy greens
Cabbages
Berries
Wild rice
Herbs and spices
Mangoes
Honeydew melon

Iron

Beans and dark green leafy vegetables are great sources of iron. Iron absorption is increased significantly by eating foods containing vitamin C along with foods containing iron.

Soybeans
Blackstrap molasses
Lentils
Spinach
Tofu
Chickpeas
Tempeh
Lima beans
Swiss chard
Collard greens
Kidney beans
Black beans
Potatoes
Quinoa
Tahini
Peas
Cashews
Bok choy
Raisins
Dried apricots
Watermelon
Almonds
Kale
Sunflower seeds
Brussels sprouts

Acknowledgments

Writing this book proved to be one of the most exciting and intense periods of my life, and there are a few people without whom it would have never been possible.

To everyone at Houghton Mifflin Harcourt, thank you for giving me the opportunity to turn my vision into this book, and for your continuous support. A very special thank-you to my editor, Stephanie Fletcher, with whom I worked so closely on this project. Your feedback and all the work and effort you put into it were invaluable and are much appreciated.

To my agent, Charlie Brotherstone, I have so much gratitude for you believing in me for the past three years, and for always being encouraging and the best agent I could have ever asked for. None of this would have happened without you.

To designer Laura Palese, thank you for turning this book into such a beautiful piece of art. Thanks also to Jonathan Castro for creating handmade ceramics to accompany the recipes.

To Jessica Almeida, thank you for everything. You're not only an integral part of the Vegan Reset family, but you've also shown me what true friendship really looks like. I'm glad we have each other, and I'll never be able to thank you enough for always being there.

To my family, Maman and John, we've lost everything together, but I believe that it made us that much stronger. Thank you for being there for me since day one, and for teaching me about what really matters in life. You are everything to me. *Je vous aime.* To Jelani, thank you for being my best friend and more than I could have ever wished for.

Last but not least, this book was written in memory of my father, who I wish I could have saved. I hope that it inspires those who feel as hopeless as he did to believe in themselves and believe that they are worthy of change. There's a Rumi quote that'll always remind me of him: *"Out beyond ideas of wrongdoing and rightdoing, there is a field. I'll meet you there."*

Index

INDEX